SOCIO-PHYSICS

EXPANDED EDITION

SOCIO-PHYSICS
APPLYING THE NATURAL SCIENCES TO CRIMINAL JUSTICE AND PENOLOGY

EXPANDED EDITION

CURTIS AND MICHELLE BLAKELY

ACADEMICA PRESS

BETHESDA - DUBLIN - PALO ALTO

Library of Congress Cataloguing-in-Publication Data

Library of Congress registration is pending

ISBN is 9781680530-24-7

Academica Press, LLC

Box 60728

Cambridge Station

Palo Alto, CA. 94306

Website: www.academicapress.com

to order: 650-329-0685

This book is dedicated to those students and scholars long forgotten.
Though our memory may fade, your efforts, contributions and discoveries persist.

CONTENTS

PREFACE

This book began to take form a number of years ago shortly after our arrivals at Truman State University. As Missouri's highly selective liberal arts and sciences college, Truman has worked tirelessly to promote effective education. Although each of us has taught for a number of years, it has taken this unique university to show us the true nature and value of undergraduate instruction. At no other time during our educational careers have we seen a faculty that more fully supports one another in their various pursuits. Here at Truman, professors and students are engaged in a relationship whereby each learns from the other and collaboration flourishes. While we have always considered teaching to be a privilege and of the highest calling, it is here that we have become most comfortable in our role as educators. We have come to see ourselves as part of a family that takes pride in offering one of the best educational values in the nation. In fact, the approach taken here at Truman has been emulated across the country, yet no other educational institution has been able to achieve the results that have popularly become known as the Truman experience. Truman's continuing reign as the best master's level public institution in the Midwest attests to this statement as does its recent recognition as the highest ranked master's level university in the United States.

A core value at Truman is interdisciplinary thinking. It is a buzz-phrase that we have come to hear frequently. Influenced by this ideological orientation, we began to look at the fields of criminal justice and in particular penology a bit differently. As social scientists, we began to increasingly wonder if biology, physics and criminal justice could be joined in a way that might increase our understanding of human and institutional behavior. We were convinced that any approach that promises to do so has a value that cannot be dismissed regardless of how absurd it may initially appear. Yes, the approaches that are undertaken within the pages that follow, while unorthodox, are intended to promote the innovative, creative, and critical thinking skills of the reader.

As the ideas contained herein were evolving, we were afforded the opportunity to visit Princeton University and the Institute for Advanced Study, both of which were Albert Einstein's old stomping grounds. Having studied Einstein's life for a number of years and being avid collectors of Einstein artifacts, this trip proved especially fruitful. We walked the same routes that he had walked. We saw the same views that he had seen, and we entered Fuld Hall just as he frequently did. We also visited one of the most scientifically minded communities on earth - Los Alamos, New Mexico. It was there that J. Robert Oppenheimer and other great scientists unraveled the mysteries of the atom based largely upon insights provided by Einstein. Their collective efforts are credited with ending World War II.

Our interest in physics has brought us into contact with researchers at the Einstein Papers Project (Caltech) and with others who have either met or have worked in close proximity to Einstein, giving us an increased appreciation for the natural sciences and their applicability to the social realm. Hereafter when we make reference to Einstein, we are in all probability doing so generically, using his name to invoke the importance of science and innovative thinking. Our visit to Princeton impressed upon us his humanity as well as his ability to see processes and events in new and exciting ways. This is exactly what we are attempting to do herein. We wish to present penology in a new way that has not yet been undertaken and to do so in a manner that helps reinvigorate it as a field of study.

Having been involved with the criminal justice system for nearly three decades now, one fact is inescapable, justice related research and the scholarship that it has produced has largely gone unchanged. This scholarship has been recycled and republished to the point that its value is negligible. To a large extent and with few exceptions, this field is growing increasingly stagnate with fewer innovative and creative insights, ideas and suggestions surfacing each year. We place the responsibility for this on the shoulders of a professorate that is becoming increasingly intolerant in their acceptance of any approach that is not firmly grounded in statistical analyses. Many colleges and universities have similarly embraced an approach whereby unorthodox and controversial approaches are actively discouraged, hindering our ability as a nation to think in new and innovative ways. This hesitancy appears to stand in stark contrast to the fact that criminal justice is a relatively young discipline, dating to the late sixties and the efforts of President Lyndon B. Johnson. As a young field, it should be chock-full of interesting and controversial ideas. However, it is not! Having come to this conclusion, we have promised our students that we would provide them with insights that would prove to be as innovative, creative and as original as possible, and we have kept this promise to the utmost of our ability. To this end, we have expanded our original book and have included two new chapters - the first dealing with evolutionary science and the second dealing with chaos. The addition of these two chapters is intended to help students develop a more comprehensive understanding of the interconnectedness of the social and natural sciences.

As you read this book, please keep several items in mind. First, the acquisition of knowledge and the development of effective problem solving skills require that one submit to new ideas and ways of thinking. An interdisciplinary approach accomplishes these objectives by creating the basis upon which seemingly divergent fields are linked. These linkages, when successful, provide added insight into human behavior. While the linkages that appear hereafter are not offered as proof that human or institutional behavior is shaped by anything other than free will, they nonetheless shed insight (even if only conceptually and/or theoretically) on those factors that should be considered when confronting problems, especially those plaguing the prison. And finally, academic pursuits need not be gravely serious or stuffy as is evidenced in the following pages.

ACKNOWLEDGEMENTS

To the Fab Five (Lynde, Jenny, Curtis, Courtland and Julianne), you have provided us with an untold measure of joy and support and have given meaning to our lives. We love each of you. While our pursuits have often resulted in failure, we have nonetheless remained secure in our hope for a bright future. It is our desire that each of you will recognize the power of persistence, remembering that slow and steady wins the race!

We thank our parents (Roger and Lillian and Johnnie and Maureen) for instilling within us the value of education. Without their influence and support, there is no telling where either of us may have ended up. As they knew, and as we have come to understand, the real value of a homemade rocket or ramjet engine is not in the thrust that it produces but in its ability to liberate one's imagination. Imagination is the key ingredient to all innovative, creative and progressive thought! After all, imagination is what fuels exploration and discovery.

We would also like to thank the many students who have inspired us throughout the years, we hope the best for each of you. You continue to remind us of the transformative nature of education. While we may have forgotten names and faces, each of you has nonetheless made our careers a continuing source of joy. It was a privilege to have worked alongside you!

CHAPTER ONE
The Prison: An Institution in Crisis

Few institutions have a greater effect on the well being of society. So when the prison is in crisis, society isn't far behind.

Upon reviewing the history of the American prison it is evident that few substantive differences exist between the early and modern correctional facility. In fact, the contemporary prison closely resembles those that were in use a century ago with few changes occurring in its design or operation. After all, the prison's most basic objective is and has always been to securely hold a captive population. The accomplishment of this objective requires little change or innovation. This is precisely why historical and contemporary prisons closely resemble one another. Prison operators also continue to rely more heavily upon time honored tradition and well-entrenched policies and procedures than on innovative or creative thinking. Of those procedural differences that have been undertaken, most have resulted from recent court cases and legislation. External influences rather than an internal impetus are responsible for those changes that have occurred. For example, one external factor that is rapidly changing the prison is increased sentence lengths. Lengthier sentences have been undertaken with little regard for how they impact the prison/prisoner. Popular enhancement laws including "three strikes-you're out" have helped create prisons that are overcrowded, violent, and devoid of therapeutic programming. These characteristics combined with high recidivism rates (recidivism is a measure of continued criminality) suggest a need to reevaluate our current use of incarceration. The prison is now in crisis!

The acknowledgement that the prison is in a state of crisis, and has been for nearly three decades, has produced a great deal of debate about its operational objectives. On one side of this debate are those who believe the primary mission of the prison is the incapacitation, control and punishment of the offender. These individuals support current judicial and legislative practices that increasingly employ incarceration as a criminal sanction. They also largely deny that a crisis even exists. On the other side of this debate are those who believe offender rehabilitation should be the primary purpose of the prison. These individuals view treatment as a requisite for a safer society. Accordingly, they assert that offender rehabilitation will lead to decreases in prison crowding, institutional and societal violence, and offender recidivism. While each group is confident in its position, it appears socially advantageous for the prison to pursue both punitive and treatment objectives simultaneously. Pursuing one of these objectives while ignoring the other is intuitively unwise since each seeks to alter the post release behavior of the offender, albeit in a different manner. In essence, punishment absent a rehabilitative rationale becomes a dehumanizing and oppressive pursuit; rehabilitation absent the corrective and deterrent-producing properties of punishment may fail to provide an incentive for personal change.

Our Correctional Pendulum

Incarceration may aptly be compared to the actions of a hypothetical pendulum. This pendulum, which reflects our nation's correctional ideology, has punishment located to one of its sides and rehabilitation to the other. The problem with this pendulum is that it sits on an uneven base. This routinely causes the pendulum's bob to favor one ideology more strongly than it does the other. During those times when our pendulum's bob reflects a pro-punishment sentiment, innovative and creative penal thought and practice becomes passé. Conversely, when a reform ideology is favored, innovative and creative thoughts become more prevalent. With this being said, it becomes apparent that an abandonment of rehabilitation by our nation's political leaders has had a corresponding effect on the prison's operations and its guiding ideology.

When considering scholarship spanning the past century, it is evident that a significant body of literature exists about penal objectives and in particular the need for balance among correctional ideologies. However, as the twenty-first century approached, scholarship began to increasingly emphasize punishment to the near exclusion of rehabilitation. This shift in ideology is reflected in the enormous number of prisons being built during this period. From 1980 to 2000, state prison construction skyrocketed. Correctional expenditures increased from approximately $12 billion per year to over $60 billion annually. It was during this era that our hypothetical pendulum's bob began to swing away from rehabilitation and toward a punitive ideology. This resulted in a prisoner population that grew so large that it made the United States the world's leading user of incarceration, placing us well ahead of both China and the former Soviet-bloc nations. In fact, the number of state and federal inmates increased from about 250,000 in 1980 to approximately 1,400,000 in 2000 (this excludes jail inmates). This increase destabilized the prison causing it to experience a dramatic rise in the number of riots occurring during this time.

Contemporary scholarship about correctional ideology and operational objectives reflect confusion about the prison's overall purpose. For example, scholars often ignore the prison's traditional objectives and fail to provide a well-reasoned discussion about each objective's merits. These scholars blatantly disregard history and refuse to acknowledge that rehabilitation traditionally formed the cornerstone of the prison's operations and was fully supported by the populace. In 1968, *Time Magazine* published a report in which more than 75% of respondents identified the prison's primary purpose as rehabilitation. However, reform ideology and public sentiment have been ignored by our political officials.

While an interest in rehabilitation has roots dating to colonial America, contemporary political support remains contentious. This is due to a government that continues to express doubts about the prison's ability to rehabilitate inmates. When these doubts are combined with budgetary deficits accruing from massive prison populations, the result tends to be a reduction in most non-essential services. For example, in at least twenty-five states, prison officials have cut or altogether eliminated educational curriculum. These reductions have resulted in fewer inmates participating in treatment. Incarceration absent treatment has now become commonplace. Referred to as warehousing and no-frills incarceration, this approach offers inmates few opportunities for educational, vocational or therapeutic betterment. This has led to elevated recidivism rates. Recent studies reveal that half of all inmates return to prison within three years of release, yet only a fifth of those who have participated in treatment return. This difference suggests that warehousing is doing little to promote public safety. Yet, the call for incarceration remains popular among politicians who wish to promote a get-tough image. In spite of these developments, not all prison systems have completely abandoned a reform ideology. Treatment, rehabilitation and offender reintegration remain thematic objectives in about half of the mission statements of departments nationwide. Even the term "corrections" which is synonymous with prison and probation efforts, suggests an attempt by some authorities to remain publicly aligned with a treatment orientation even when doing so is politically unpopular. This suggests a disjunction between what politicians believe the prison's objectives to be and what some correctional officials and citizens expect the prison to achieve.

"What if…?"

It is often beneficial to consider alternative views when seeking a fresh perspective on one's own areas of interest - and whose views are better to consider than the quintessential scholar himself, Albert Einstein? Einstein, perhaps the most celebrated of all physicists, never had a laboratory, a telescope or any of the other tools common to his discipline. Instead, he sought answers to the most perplexing scientific questions of our time by using little more than pen, paper and a great deal of innovative and creative thought. He was an expert at conducting thought experiments. Thought experiments are mental exercises where one seeks to answer the question "what-if?" without actually engaging in a physical experiment. Instead, the experiment is conducted within the mind of the scholar, with past experience and logic providing an answer about the probable outcome. On one occasion when asked about his laboratory's whereabouts, Einstein removed a pen from his breast pocket and exclaimed "here". Such a response suggests that pricey equipment and complicated statistical analyses are not prerequisites for discovery. Instead, Einstein suggested that advancements are produced through innovative and creative thought. Furthermore, he often declared that "God doesn't play dice with the universe" when explaining that complex interactions are governed by universal laws and not by happenstance. Immanuel Kant, a German philosopher whose writings influenced Einstein, also recognized the value of creative and innovative thought. Kant believed that solutions to most problems could be found in personal and collective experience. Kant was also suggesting, albeit in a less direct manner, the use of the thought experiment. Both of these great thinkers recognized that the question "what if…?" naturally stimulates thought processes that are necessary to produce solutions. The "what if?" question continues to shape the work of many scientists. In fact, in a recent movie adaptation of H.G. Wells' novel *The Time Machine* it was noted that this question has always driven humankind's quest for knowledge. While the prison doesn't easily submit itself to the rigors of scientific experimentation, penologists may nonetheless liberally apply the thought experiment. By asking "what if…?" and mentally formulating the likely answer or answers to this question, penologists are able to devise solutions to the prison's many challenges.

Admittedly, physics, philosophy and penology are quite different disciplines. However, we remain confident that if more academicians were to embrace Einstein and Kant's thought experiments and rely more heavily upon innovative and creative thought, American penology would benefit. Innovative and creative thought would permit us to approach challenges in new and exciting ways, potentially allowing academicians and practitioners to devise solutions to some of the most pressing problems facing the prison. One solution that promises to restore an ideological balance to contemporary operations while reducing crowding, violence and recidivism is prison specialization. Specialization refers to classifying inmates based, in part, on their interest in treatment. Inmates are either willing to participate in therapeutic initiatives or they are not. Once classified, inmates are grouped accordingly and are then placed into separate prisons (or different areas of the same institution) designed to meet the specific needs of each group. By eliminating interaction between these two groups, those who desire treatment can pursue it freely in a supportive and nurturing environment. In typical Einstein fashion, specialization seeks to relegate happenstance to the periphery of institutional operations by attempting to make correctional intervention and intra-prison relationships more deliberate, supportive and productive.

The Historical Basis of Prison Specialization

Before describing specialization in greater detail, it is important to recognize that its foundations are historically based. Early within U.S. history, citizens sought a way to protect weak, impressionable and less assertive inmates from those prisoners who were more predatory in nature. This desire eventually resulted in the separation of inmates based on age and gender. Proposals promoting specialization are based upon these earlier practices and seek to separate inmates according to their desire to undergo treatment. The separation of those who desire treatment from those who do not would effectively eliminate the opportunity for the hardened and predatory inmate to coerce, intimidate or otherwise victimize those who are more malleable. This proposed separation is based upon the probability that the more experienced and hardened offender will corrupt those who are less criminally inclined. Inmates who are good prospects for reform are at particular risk since it is the more experienced inmate who controls the prison's culture. By separating these two groups, the less experienced and more impressionable inmate would be shielded from the corrupting influence of those inmates who oppose therapeutic processes. Perhaps the most ardent supporter of specialization was Howard Gill (a twentieth century penologist and the first superintendent of the Norfolk Prison Colony in Massachusetts). Gill asserted that inmate demeanor should be a consideration of the modern correctional practitioner. Gill's proposal for prison specialization suggests that:

- a diversity exists among the inmate population about the perceived value of treatment,
- some inmates desire treatment while others do not,
- it must be determined into which group each inmate belongs,
- based on this determination, each group should be housed within its own prison (or in separate areas of the same prison) just as we now separate delinquents from adult offenders and female offenders from their male counterparts, and
- separation of this nature protects the integrity of treatment processes and increases the likelihood for inmate reform.

For our purposes, inmate demeanor is of two varieties, it either reflects an interest in treatment (amenable) or it reflects little or no interest (nonamenable). Recognizing this difference, specialized prisons can be created to deliver focused treatment based upon the assertion that amenable inmates, if not housed separately, will be manipulated and exploited by those inmates who are more criminally inclined. If left to such a fate, any desire on their part to undergo treatment and pursue personal reform may forever be lost. Similarly, it is recognized that it is unnecessary for nonamenable inmates to be afforded treatment since to do so would be improper, financially irresponsible and would fail to contribute to the betterment of society.

The separation of these two groups is based on the probability that nonamenable inmates often adhere to a preemptive mode of action that results in their use of threats, coercion and violence against those perceived as being pro-treatment. This approach when used against the amenable inmate population discourages participation in therapeutic programming. The Honorable Winston Churchill, when serving as the British Home Secretary (1910-1911) (an office responsible for dealing with crime and disorder in England and Wales) sought to improve the certainty of offender reform by separating amenable offenders from those who might exert a corrupting influence. Churchill's call for reform was later endorsed by Sir Walter Buchanan (Inspector-General of Prisons in the Presidency of Bengal) when he commented on the need to create a specialized prison system within the United States as a means to reduce negativity and the corrupting effect of peer pressure (1921). Peer pressure is a pervasive force that is exerted upon an individual to conform to a group's values and behavioral code. While a desire to conform may be internally driven, it is most often seen as an external force that is applied to an individual by those in a position to shape behavior. If an inmate resists conformity, questions about his or her loyalty may arise. Questions of this nature can quickly result in an inmate's injury and death, so conformity is often considered a necessary self-protective measure.

Peer Pressure

It should come as no surprise that the contemporary inmate culture is characterized by a pervasive form of peer pressure that seeks to meld a diverse population into a unified whole. The purpose of this unification is to protect inmate interests against what is perceived to be an overly oppressive and unjust system. This approach makes it possible for the inmate population to act in collective opposition to the rules and procedures established by the institution's administration. The negative effects of peer pressure have long been recognized. For example, parental admonitions have cautioned an untold number of youth about the need to choose friends wisely. We have witnessed countless times when a similar warning is given to new inmates by correctional employees urging them to carefully select their institutional associates. Warnings of this kind suggest that one's peers can and do influence behavior. Such an acknowledgement suggests that:

- individuals tend to internalize the values and characteristics of their associates,
- negative associations tend to produce negative behaviors while positive associations tend to produce positive behaviors,
- a pro-crime/anti-social attitude is encouraged in the contemporary prison where negative peer pressure thrives, and
- negative peer pressure can have a corrupting influence on the impressionable inmate, thereby perpetuating criminality.

The power of peer pressure is affirmed within the pages of most social science textbooks. In the field of psychology, numerous theories are used to explain human behavior. However, we will only present two that appear especially applicable. The first of these is the behaviorist view which asserts that the human mind is a blank slate and that behavior is largely learned within one's environment. If one encounters positive and nurturing people within that environment, one's behavior is also likely to be (or become) positive and nurturing. However, if one's environment is characterized by negativity and predatory behavior, one's own behaviors may become negative and predatory in nature. It is within the environment where values and thought processes are modeled and imitated. Typically, the inmate population displays a continuum of problematic behaviors which collectively create a toxic culture. This culture, in turn, celebrates and promotes criminality. Furthermore, since inmates outnumber staff and since the prison is an isolating and a socially isolated institution, its culture is almost exclusively shaped by inmates. This has produced jungle like environments where nonamenable inmates can freely corrupt those who are less assertive and less criminally experienced.

The humanistic view (another psychological perspective) considers how self-perceptions affect behavior. This approach suggests that human action is shaped by rewards and reinforcements. For example, to ensure the proper mental and emotional development of children, it is necessary that they receive positive reinforcement and adult approval. When positive reinforcements are provided, proper and socially approved behaviors tend to become normative. However, when praise and approval are withheld, self-image and one's perceived worth may be adversely affected. Feelings of defeat and a poor self-image may lead to a repeating and worsening of problematic behaviors. In essence, an unhealthy environment can have an adverse effect on one's development and subsequent behavior. In the prison, which may be viewed as an unhealthy and hostile environment, opportunities for positive growth and development are limited as is one's ability to avoid negative influences. This may lead to criminal orientations that ultimately become more ingrained.

Concerns about the relationship between peer pressure and imprisonment are warranted since inmates tend to internalize the prison's culture to such an extent that it often becomes firmly affixed. This process, referred to as institutionalization or prisonization explains many of the behavioral problems exhibited by former inmates. While psychological views increase our understanding of how peer pressure and environment can negatively shape behavior, they similarly suggest that positive peer pressure and a nurturing environment could be used to minimize or altogether eliminate the harmful effects of incarceration.

Let us now turn our attention toward two sociological perspectives that are relevant for our examination. We will begin by considering the concept of social ecology. According to this perspective, environments (described as communities) are comparable to living organisms and like all living organisms, evolve, adapt and can become sick. As this approach was being developed, researchers found that Chicago (where studies were being conducted) consisted of various zones resembling the concentric circles of a target. As immigrant groups were arriving at the turn of the twentieth century, economic hardships forced them to live near the city's center in squalor conditions. As the economic situation of each respective group improved, it would vacate a particular zone in an attempt to place distance between itself and the city's center. With distance came an increase in quality of life - the greater the distance from the city's center, the more dramatic the improvement. As this occurred, each group would then be replaced by a new one. Regardless of differences in race, ethnicity or nationality, crime rates remained stable in these transitional zones. This finding suggested that crime rates were not a characteristic of a factor unique to any particular group, but were instead linked to conditions found within these environments. One's environment was seen as a crucial determinant in behavior. To explain this, the concept of cultural transmission evolved. Cultural transmission asserts that criminality is transmitted to individuals via environment through processes of communication and interaction. This suggests that a community's culture can become so ingrained that it influences behavior.

There are additional theories that specifically assert that criminal behavior is learned through interactions with one's friends and family. Learning theories suggest that impressionable individuals tend to imitate the behaviors of those with whom they interact. Imitation is a significant component of the learning process and just as some individuals learn conventional behaviors by imitation some also learn criminality. The latter involves both the techniques and attitudes necessary for the commission of crime. Criminal behavior is also influenced by the frequency, intensity and duration of the contact that occurs between an individual and his/her peer group. One's peer group often plays a significant role in behavior since normal maturation processes tend to decrease familial influence. Of course, those peers having the most frequent, the most intense, and the longest lasting contact with an individual will exert greater influence over behavior than will those whose contact is less frequent, less intense and is shorter in duration. Interestingly enough, this effect may be magnified in the prison since it is difficult for inmates to escape membership in the dominant culture. Since peer contact within a penal setting is frequent, intense and prolonged, the probability for a transfer of criminogenic values increases. Future crimes by former inmates may then be partially attributable to attitudes developed during a previous incarceration. Since the processes of learning conformity and criminality are identical, with modification the prison could become more effective in promoting offender reform. Furthermore, all learning processes involve the application of rewards and punishments. For example, behaviors that are desired by one's peers are rewarded whereas undesirable behaviors are discouraged. Impressionable inmates have little choice but to associate with a populace that is largely controlled by those who are more experienced and powerful. By embracing the prison's culture, amenable inmates win acceptance. This acceptance is a reward for acting in a manner consistent with the expectations of inmate leaders. Conversely, a rejection of this culture may result in censure, ostracism, assault and even death.

Finally, we should consider the possibility that criminals and noncriminals share a similar set of values. It has long been asserted that all offenders ascribe to those values that are promoted by larger society. These conventional values reflect a consensus about acceptable behaviors. Criminal values are those that stand in opposition to this consensus, violating society's laws and negatively impacting public safety. Criminals tend to adhere to conventional values a majority of the time but occasionally choose to indulge in criminal activities when doing so is personally beneficial. In essence, offenders "drift" between these two value-sets depending on which set proves more advantageous at a particular time. One set of values may, given the right circumstances, become dominant. Since incarceration tends to isolate inmates from conventional values and beliefs, criminal values and beliefs may become more deeply ingrained. During incarceration, conventional values may lose their significance and be replaced by those that are of a pro-crime orientation. More importantly, if offenders tend to ascribe to conventional values, then it stands to reason that these values, if given an opportunity, could be strengthened through positive peer influence, treatment, and by protecting impressionable inmates from the corrupting influence of those who are more criminally inclined.

Conclusion

The body of literature existing prior to 1980 affirms rehabilitation as a penal pursuit. While current political posturing de-emphasizes rehabilitation by raising questions about the effectiveness of treatment, the fact remains that nearly all inmates will eventually return to society. We must, therefore, acknowledge that current practices do little to promote public safety on any meaningful or lasting basis.

Perspectives based in the social sciences suggest that attempts at offender reform will continue to be ineffective not because inmates as a group are unable or even unwilling to change but because officials continue to house amenable and nonamenable inmates within the same institutions. This practice guarantees that cross contamination will continue. Cross contamination can be visualized as the process by which amenable inmates become nonamenable due to the negative influences found within the prison's larger culture. Until the prison's culture is made more supportive and nurturing, the amenable inmate will not reach his/her fullest potential nor will the prison live up to the expectations of the taxpayer.

Ultimately, the value in considering prison specialization is twofold. First, it serves as the basis for inquiry into prison operations. An open discourse about the prison is necessary if we are to enhance public safety. Secondly, such a proposal provides a remedy for many of the prison's shortcomings. If negative peer pressure can prevent amenable inmates from seeking treatment, and if a pro-crime culture exists within our prisons, then measures can be implemented to correct these problems. In doing so, the integrity and effectiveness of treatment processes could be improved.

The need remains, as it has for many years, for change to occur within the prison. By assessing each inmate's demeanor toward treatment and by shielding the amenable inmate from the corrupting influences of those who may disrupt therapeutic processes, recidivism rates might decrease. It is conceivable that future prisons could be modified to make them more effective in reforming the amenable inmate population. Action based upon thought, observation and theory would improve a system that appears hesitant to embrace innovative and progressive ideals. By pursuing punishment and rehabilitation simultaneously, the bob of our hypothetical pendulum would again swing evenly, reflecting an ideological balance. Perhaps contemporary penologists could learn something from Einstein, Kant and Churchill. Their examples clearly reflect the value of innovative and creative thought. And as Einstein reminds us, "God doesn't play dice with the universe" nor should penologists allow happenstance to govern modern prison operations. Instead we should ensure that amenable inmates are given the opportunity to achieve a reformed state without hindrance or fear of retaliation.

In the next chapter, the prison is compared to a living organism with particular attention being paid to its equilibrium, growth, health and evolution. Peer pressure stemming from an overly negative inmate culture is seen as perpetuating the crime cycle rather than serving to break it. Attention is also paid to the relationship existing between the amenable and nonamenable inmate population and prison specialization.

HIGHLIGHTS

- The contemporary prison closely resembles those that were in use a century ago with few changes occurring in its design or operation.

- When technological advances are discounted, few substantive differences exist between early and modern prisons.

- Prison operators have been slow to adopt innovative practices, relying instead on time-honored tradition and well-entrenched policies and procedures.

- Popular enhancement laws including "three-strikes you're out" have helped to create prisons that are overcrowded, violent and devoid of therapeutic programming.

- It appears socially advantageous for the prison to pursue both punitive and treatment objectives simultaneously. Pursuing one of these objectives while ignoring the other is intuitively unwise since each seeks to alter the post-release behavior of the offender.

- During those times when our nation's correctional ideology reflects a pro-punishment sentiment, innovative and creative thought and practice becomes passé. Conversely when a reform ideology is favored, innovative and creative thoughts become more prevalent.

- From 1980 to 2000, state prison construction skyrocketed. Likewise, correctional expenditures increased from approximately $12 billion per year to over $60 billion annually.

- Increased prisoner populations destabilized the prison which experienced a dramatic increase in the number of riots occurring during the last few decades of the twentieth century.

- The prison's effectiveness and its social value should be determined by a diminishing need for its services, not by the size of its inmate population. In essence, the prison should seek to put itself out of business.

- Incarceration absent a rehabilitative rationale becomes a dehumanizing and oppressive pursuit; rehabilitation absent the corrective properties of punishment may fail to produce an incentive for personal change.

- Incarceration absent an attempt at treatment has now become commonplace. Referred to as warehousing and no-frills incarceration, this approach offers inmates few opportunities for educational, vocational or therapeutic betterment.
- Contemporary scholarship reflects confusion about the prison's objectives and overall purpose.
- While an interest in offender reform has its roots dating to colonial America, modern attempts at treatment remain contentious.
- A call for the increased use of incarceration as a criminal sanction remains popular among politicians who wish to promote a tough image.
- One might speculate that the term "corrections" misrepresents what is actually occurring within the prison, that this misrepresentation is intentional and that it serves to promote the interest of those in power.
- It proves fruitful to consider alternative views when searching for a fresh perspective on one's own areas of interest.
- Thought experiments are mental exercises where one seeks to answer the question of "what if…?" without actually engaging in a physical experiment. Instead the experiment is conducted within the mind of the scholar, with past experience and logic providing an answer about the probable outcome.
- Amenable inmates are at risk for exploitation, victimization and manipulation by those who are more hardened, predatory and experienced.
- Prison specialization refers to classifying inmates based, in part, on their interest in treatment. Once classified, inmates are grouped accordingly and are then placed into separate prisons (or different areas of the same institution) designed to meet the specific needs of each group.
- Inmate demeanor is of two varieties, it either reflects an interest in treatment (amenable) or it reflects little or no interest (nonamenable).
- We should, by intelligent and deliberate design, ensure that amenable inmates are given the opportunity to achieve a reformed state without hindrance or fear of retaliation.

- Peer pressure is a pervasive force that is exerted upon an individual to conform to a group's values and behavioral code. It is an external force that is applied to an individual by those in a position to influence behavior.

- It should come as no surprise that the contemporary inmate culture is characterized by a pervasive form of peer pressure that seeks to meld a diverse population into a unified whole.

- In the prison, which may be viewed as an unhealthy and hostile environment, opportunities for positive growth and development are limited as is one's ability to avoid negativity.

- Since inmates outnumber staff and since the prison is a socially-isolated institution, its culture is almost exclusively shaped by inmates. This has produced a jungle like environment where nonamenable inmates can freely corrupt those who are less experienced.

- Negative associations tend to produce negative behaviors while positive associations tend to produce positive behaviors.

- Concerns about the relationship between peer pressure and imprisonment gain considerable significance when one acknowledges that institutional and post-release behaviors are related.

- While psychological views increase our understanding of how peer pressure and environment can negatively shape behavior, they similarly suggest that positive peer pressure and a nurturing environment could be used to promote inmate reform, thus minimizing or altogether eliminating the harmful effects of incarceration.

- Cultural transmission asserts that criminality is transmitted to individuals via environment through processes of communication and interaction. This suggests that the culture present in any particular environment can become so ingrained within its residents that it influences behavior.

- Those inmates who are impressionable tend to imitate the behaviors of those with whom they interact. Imitation is a significant component of the learning process and just as some individuals learn conventional behaviors by imitation some also learn criminality.

- Criminal behavior is influenced by the frequency, intensity and duration of the contact that occurs between an individual and his/her peers.

- Since the process of learning conformity and criminality is identical, with modification the prison could become more effective in promoting offender reform.

- Impressionable inmates have little choice but to associate with a populace that is largely controlled by those offenders who are more experienced and powerful.

- By embracing the prison's culture, inmates win acceptance. This acceptance is a reward for acting in a manner consistent with the expectations of inmate leaders. Conversely, a rejection of this culture may result in censure, ostracism, assault and even death.

- Criminals tend to adhere to conventional values a majority of the time but occasionally choose to indulge in criminal activities when doing so proves personally beneficial.

- Since incarceration tends to isolate inmates from conventional values, criminal values may become more deeply ingrained.

- If offenders ascribe to conventional values then it stands to reason that these values, if given an opportunity, could be strengthened through positive peer influence, treatment and by protecting impressionable inmates from the corrupting influence of those that are more criminally-inclined.

- Attempts at offender reform will continue to be ineffective not because inmates as a group are unable or even unwilling to change, but because officials continue to house amenable and nonamenable inmates within the same institutions.

QUESTIONS

1). How has the prison changed over the past century? Have these changes had a direct impact on the prison's operational objectives? Why or why not? Explain.

2). The observation was made that when a reform ideology is favored by the political establishment, innovative and creative thought flourishes, but when punishment is favored, these thoughts are discouraged. Is this an accurate observation? Explain.

3). What value is there in the "what if…?" question and when/how should it be applied to correctional operations?

4). What are the characteristics of the inmate culture? Does this culture value rehabilitation? Why or why not? How is participation in therapeutic programs either encouraged or discouraged by this culture? Explain.

5). Should those inmates who desire treatment be separated from those who do not? Explain.

6). Is the term "corrections" misleading? What does this term suggest? Is the correcting of offenders an active or a passive process? Explain.

7). Is it accurate to suggest that since the prison is a socially isolated institution, its culture is almost exclusively shaped by inmates? Explain. Assuming this to be a correct observation, what effect might this have upon the overall operations of a prison and on the likelihood that treatment programs will be adequately attended? Explain.

8). Are those behaviors that an inmate displays during incarceration suggestive of what his/her behaviors will be upon release? Similarly, are those values that an inmate ascribes to during incarceration related to those that he/she will espouse when paroled or discharged? Explain.

9). Would treatment provided in a positive and nurturing environment promote inmate reform? Explain. Could such an environment be created and promoted within the contemporary prison? Explain.

10). Why would an amenable inmate embrace a culture characterized by negativity and violence? If he/she were to reject this culture would there be consequences? Would an acceptance of this culture affect an inmate's future propensity to commit crime? Explain.

CHAPTER TWO
A Living Organism

A sick institution begets sick individuals.
Physician, heal thyself!

In the previous chapter we began to use Albert Einstein's approach, among others, to seek a greater understanding of institutional and human behavior. Einstein frequently asserted that all events are the direct and predictable result of universal laws, implying an inherent responsibility among scientists to discover and understand these laws. Similarly, we believe that penologists have an inherent responsibility to discover and understand the principles that govern the prison's operations. The achievement of this objective would allow us to improve the prison's ability to promote public safety.

As we became familiar with Einstein's work, we realized that an interdisciplinary investigation beginning with a biological perspective might prove both interesting and insightful. In arriving at this conclusion, we considered the position taken by the Vienna Circle, an early twentieth century group of philosopher-scientists. The members of this group advocated a doctrine of interdisciplinary study and unification through which all science would share a common set of laws, methods and language. Additional support for our approach was found in the observations of Freeman Dyson, an award winning mathematician and physicist, who similarly suggests that all efforts at discovery must begin with a consideration of biology. Surely, if these scientists recognized a value in considering their fields from an interdisciplinary and biological framework, perhaps we should as well. As we began to contemplate a possible connection between biology and penology, we formed an appreciation for the plethora of avenues it affords in furthering penal discourse. For example, when using terms that include contamination and contagion, we are referring to a process that while generally viewed as biological in nature has social applications as well. For our consideration, these words represent the process by which pro-crime and antisocial attitudes are reinforced and perpetuated within the prison. While a social contagion isn't biologically based, it nonetheless has a detrimental effect on the values, beliefs and behaviors of inmates.

A conceptual approach based on biology finds its origins in the Chicago School of Thought, which emerged during the early twentieth century and refers to a group of sociologists working at the University of Chicago. Faculty affiliated with this school included such luminaries as Ernest Burgess, Everett Hughes, Frederick Clements, Robert Park and Edwin Sutherland. These researchers dominated sociological and criminological scholarship of the period, often writing from a biologically-based perspective. This approach eventually led them to compare various Chicago communities to living organisms, postulating that community health is affected by social conditions. It is these social conditions that either promote or hinder the safety and security of the citizenry. When applied to a penal setting, this view suggests that a prison's state of health can have a dramatic effect on an inmate's post release behavior. In essence, a healthy prison that promotes personal responsibility, treatment and rehabilitation would impact post release behavior much differently than a prison that devalues treatment and is characterized by idleness and predation. Viewed from this perspective, the prison is comparable to other communities; yet the degree of influence the prison exerts over its residents' behaviors may exceed that which occurs in society. The strength of this influence may be found in its pervasive and unique form of peer pressure. While we will return shortly to the Chicago School of Thought, for now simply entertain the possibility that the prison's culture may actually perpetuate criminality, which is of course counterproductive to its mission.

Peer Pressure and Behavior

It appears appropriate to begin this section by observing that inmates are proficient at creating and perpetuating a culture of peer pressure that promotes opposition to all non-inmate authority. This culture requires that inmates demonstrate loyalty to one another and to their leaders. A principal requirement of this culture is the withholding of information from the prison's authorities while opposing correctional intervention in all of its various forms including treatment. This culture regulates all interactions between inmates and between inmates and staff. However, it does not prohibit the predation of weaker inmates by those who are stronger and more criminally inclined. This culture requires that less experienced inmates bend to the will of those more criminally accomplished. This ensures that:

- inmates, especially new ones, adopt the values and behaviors of those who are more experienced,
- the adoption of these values and behaviors become normative within the prison, and
- these values and behaviors are demonstrated through a progressively hardened and calloused approach when encountering those who are weaker or who represent state authority.

The influential power of peer pressure is affirmed by a number of perspectives that directly associate it with behavior. For example, we have already considered that within the field of psychology, the behaviorist view suggests that actions are influenced by the values, norms and beliefs present within one's environment. If one's environment is comprised of positive and nurturing associates, one's behavior is likely to be positive and nurturing, but if one's environment is characterized by those exuding negativity and violence, one's behavior may also become negative and violent. And, as we have already seen, numerous social science perspectives suggest that the young and impressionable may find it especially difficult to resist the influence of a negative environment. A negative environment may lead these individuals to adopt progressively more destructive attitudes and behaviors. Consider that in the prison, inmates outnumber staff, suggesting that its culture wields a pervasive and overwhelming degree of influence. Furthermore, the prison itself is socially isolated. Collectively, these observations suggest that the prison's culture is influenced almost exclusively by powerful prisoners. These prisoners seek to create an environment that they can control, manipulate and exploit for personal gain. Since new, inexperienced and young inmates are concerned for their own safety, they are often eager to win the approval of inmate leaders. It is from this fear and uncertainty that control is derived. Such a culture is maintained through violence with dissenters being ostracized, attacked and occasionally killed.

Let us now return to our previous discussion of the Chicago School of Thought. If you recall, its researchers developed the concept of social ecology which asserts that environments share a number of characteristics in common with biological organisms. Among these similarities is the notion that communities can become sick and diseased. And interestingly enough, these researchers found that immigrant groups, upon arriving in Chicago, were forced because of economic hardships, to reside near the city's center. This area was characterized by poverty, overcrowding, a lack of personal space and deplorable living conditions. However, as each group's economic situation improved, members would vacate the innermost zones of Chicago and distance themselves from its center. As this distance increased, living conditions and quality of life improved. Since each group desired prosperity, members sought to move away from the heavily industrialized and commercialized areas of the city and out toward the suburbs. As each group slowly vacated the particular zone that it had occupied, it was replaced by a new immigrant group that was engaged in the same pursuit. Regardless of differences in group nationality or ethnicity, crime rates remained stable in these transitional zones even when one immigrant group was replaced by another. This convinced researchers that environment plays a significant role in determining behavior. This approach eventually gave credence to the notion of cultural transmission, suggesting that a community's culture is transmitted to its residents through interaction and communication. In this case, the new immigrant group came into contact with the group that it was replacing. This resulted in a transfer of the community's culture. One's length of residency becomes a primary factor in the transmission process. The longer one's exposure to a particular community the greater this effect, while conversely the shorter the exposure, the weaker the effect. The communities studied by these researchers share a number of traits in common with the prison. These traits include:

- residential turnover,
- ongoing conflict,
- relative poverty, and
- an absence of personal space and privacy.

Based upon these observations, one might surmise that prisons are fully capable of transmitting attitudes and behaviors favorable to criminality. If true, then modifying the prison's environment might noticeably disrupt transmission processes while reducing recidivism rates.

As we have previously seen, young and impressionable individuals often learn behaviors by mimicking those behaviors of their associates. The stronger the connection between an individual and his/her associates, the greater the resulting effect. This suggests that the processes by which one learns to act lawfully or criminally are identical and are influenced by the frequency, intensity and duration of contact. Therefore, those relationships having the most frequent, the most intense and the longest lasting contact, will exert a greater degree of influence over one's behavior than those relationships whose contact is less frequent, less intense and shorter in duration. When considered from a correctional perspective, this effect may be intensified within the prison since it is difficult for an inmate to escape membership in the dominant culture. Since negative contact in the prison is frequent, intense and prolonged, the transfer of criminogenic values and techniques becomes highly probable.

Rewards and punishments may also play a significant role in shaping behavior. Often referred to as stimulus-response, this perspective suggests that behaviors that are deemed desirable by one's peers will result in acceptance and privilege while those that are determined to be undesirable often result in exclusion and even retaliation. When applied to a penal setting, this perspective assumes even greater significance since young and impressionable offenders are in constant contact with those who are more criminally experienced. Since experienced inmates control the prison, less experienced offenders have little choice but to adopt their nonconformist ideology under threat of ostracism and violence.

It has also been suggested that a large percentage of offenders ascribe to conventional values. In fact, it is possible that offenders and non-offenders hold a similar set of values, with offenders engaging in conventional behaviors a majority of the time. However, drift may cause movement toward criminality. This drift can and is often affected by one's environment. For example, an individual may oscillate between conventional and nonconventional value sets, provided that no commitment has been made to adopt criminality as a permanent lifestyle choice. Not only do most offenders hold conventional values, but these values are frequently reflected in the guilt that is expressed following a criminal act. This suggests that it is a socially destructive practice to incarcerate those displaying strong conventional values with those who do not. By forcing young and inexperienced offenders into close proximity with hardened inmates, prisons throughout the United States are failing to promote pro-social values among those who are likely to be amenable toward reform. To break this destructive process, innovative and creative thought is needed.

Innovative and Creative Thought

As this chapter began to take form, we became painfully aware that some readers might be confused by our use of biology as a tool to increase understanding of penal issues. This confusion stems from the fact that no widely recognized label exists to describe such an approach. We, therefore, have taken the liberty to coin the term bio-penology. We did this in an attempt to minimize confusion about these efforts and to suggest that an understanding of the prison might be facilitated by considering it from a biological perspective.

To fully appreciate this approach, it is necessary to define penology. For our purposes we define penology as the study of the prison's operations, its culture, its objectives, and those individuals that it employs and incarcerates. Penology is an important consideration within the field of criminal justice since the prison impacts the lives of countless citizens and inmates. The manner in which our prisons operate has a direct and lasting effect on the quality of life of virtually every citizen. In spite of its influence and enormity, suggestions for improving the prison system are noticeably absent from recent scholarship. This may be due to the contemporary movement that views penology as being synonymous with punishment, paying little attention to treatment or rehabilitation. Such a mindset has undoubtedly stifled innovative and creative thought as a means to improve the efficiency and effectiveness of the prison.

While many of us are aware that biology is the study of life, the act of living is perplexingly complex. After all, what is life? We all recognize life when we see it, but it eludes a precise definition. In fact, no comprehensive definition has ever been offered. Instead, a number of characteristics are generally recognized and accepted as indicators of life. Among these are respiration, movement and metabolism. While these characteristics are not relevant to the present task and will not be considered herein, four additional characteristics are pertinent. These characteristics are homeostasis, growth, contagion and evolution. A consideration of these characteristics is important since it allows a direct comparison to be made between living organisms and penal environments. These characteristics are described as follows:

- Homeostasis is the ability of an organism to maintain a stable and healthy equilibrium. It refers to a balance that exists between all internal systems in such a way that the organism is vibrant and energetic. If homeostasis is not achieved and maintained, referred to as homeostatic imbalance, an unhealthy condition results. This condition compromises the ability of an organism to function properly.

The institutional equivalent of homeostatic imbalance is ideological imbalance which refers to an internal confusion about an organization's own objectives. This confusion makes it difficult for an institution to effectively accomplish any but its most basic goals. An organization's ideology, which is comparable to the internal, instinctual and motivational systems of an organism, when in balance, promotes operational efficiency and effectiveness. When dealing with multiple objectives, as is the case with the prison, an imbalance may occur if any particular goal loses favor or is perceived to be less achievable than the others.

There are a number of operational objectives that have long been associated with the prison. These include incapacitation, deterrence and rehabilitation. Incapacitation refers to rendering inmates incapable of further predation by temporarily removing them from society. Deterrence is the cessation of future criminality that results from a fear of being punished. This fear is believed to be the natural result of the punitive process. However, fear is increasingly being recognized as a poor motivator and should not be considered a substitute for real and lasting change. Collectively, we refer to incapacitation and deterrence as being part and parcel of a punitive ideology. While incapacitation and fear may create a short-term change in behavior, rehabilitation is the only objective that creates long-term change. This change is due to an acknowledgement that criminality is not a personally or socially constructive behavior. Furthermore, rehabilitation involves equipping inmates with the skills and knowledge necessary for their successful return to society. When rehabilitation is successfully accomplished, the crime cycle is broken.

Homeostasis within the institution represents an ideological and operational balance whereby each of the previously identified objectives is equally valued and pursued. Each of these objectives has traditionally sought to promote public safety through a unified and collective approach. However, since there appears to be an imbalance in the contemporary prison, the suggestion that institutions individually specialize in incapacitation or rehabilitation appears appropriate. Thus, some prisons could focus on incapacitation whereas others would focus their efforts on treatment and rehabilitation. This approach would more fully restore the effectiveness of correctional intervention without forsaking rehabilitation for punitive measures. Moreover, it would separate inmates based upon their amenability toward correctional intervention and would protect the integrity of treatment initiatives (more on this approach shortly).

- Growth is the tendency of an organism to increase in size over time. While growth is typically viewed as an indication of homeostasis, it does not necessarily indicate health, since unhealthy and diseased organisms also grow, and at times, growth itself is a consequence of sickness.

While the growth of the prison may be interpreted as an indication of health and vitality (from an institutional viewpoint), from a social and/or therapeutic perspective it more aptly indicates imbalance. As such, the prison's growth may result from an ideology that advocates punishment to the near exclusion of treatment and rehabilitative initiatives. Such an imbalance describes the current approach to prison management and is responsible for the substantial increase in our inmate population.

Advocates of a punitive ideology tend to embrace an orientation that is expansion-friendly. More commonly referred to as a widening of the correctional net, this approach seeks to control and punish greater numbers of our citizens. In essence, a punitive rationale naturally seeks to expand its influence, and when punishment is not counterbalanced by rehabilitative ideology (an orientation that advocates a decreasing need for correctional services), growth is the inevitable result. One might make the observation that the prison is an institution that should seek to reduce a need for its services. It is reasonable to believe that a system that embraces a treatment orientation and effectively pursues rehabilitation would contract rather than expand.

- Contagion as used herein suggests that since biological and institutional entities can exist in a state of imbalance, it stands to reason that they can also promote a similar state in others. For example, all living organisms are subject to sickness and disease. Once infected, a sickness or disease can be passed to other organisms. When dealing with prisons, we are not concerned with biological contagions; instead we are concerned with social contagions. Social contagions are those attitudes, actions and values that run counter to the health and well being of society. To prevent the spread of biological contagions, isolation or quarantine of the infected organism becomes necessary. Perhaps the same action is needed when dealing with social contagions. By separating those inmates who are amenable toward treatment from those who are not, contamination is prevented.
- Evolution refers to the ability of an organism to change in order to meet environmental challenges. Just as organisms can evolve, and in doing so often become more successful, so too can the prison. Regardless of where the prison has come from or where it is currently, it can evolve into an institution that is able to efficiently and effectively meet its public service mandate.

When considering these characteristics, it becomes obvious that each relates to the ability of an organism, and for our purposes an institution, to maintain a state of balance and health. When a state of balance and health is achieved, organisms and institutions are both able to effectively function. When a state of health is not maintained, proper functioning is compromised. Once compromised, an organism or institution loses its ability to effectively deal with the challenges it encounters.

Thus, a biological perspective suggests that if an organism loses its internal balance, it can no longer effectively function within its environment. A biological approach similarly suggests that when the prison loses its ideological balance it too becomes dysfunctional. This increases the likelihood that it will promote dysfunction among the inmate population.

The Abandonment of a Reform Ideology

The contemporary prison has largely abandoned its treatment ideology. This abandonment has resulted from, and has subsequently contributed to, a growing conservatism about how we should deal with offenders. While such a posturing has led to large inmate populations, these populations have further contributed to the abandonment of rehabilitation. The strain of nearly 2.5 million jail and prison inmates has caused correctional officials to eliminate all non-essential, non-security related services. Instead, the funds that have historically been earmarked for treatment are now being used to maintain our system's massive inmate population. The enormous cost associated with housing this population has left many correctional systems financially unprepared. For example, Connecticut, Washington State and Michigan are each currently facing correctional budget deficits well in excess of a billion dollars. These deficits have forced officials to provide no-frills incarceration where little consideration is given to the utility of educational, vocational or therapeutic initiatives.

A contemporary political posturing that fails to recognize treatment as a legitimate activity is misguided since punishment and rehabilitation have historically counterbalanced one another as institutional objectives. Punishment ensured that the prison would produce a deterrent effect while treatment helped guarantee the reform of amenable inmates. Both objectives working in unison served to promote public safety. A growing conservatism that began to gain momentum in the 1970s resulted in the construction of a massive number of prisons and an inmate population that has grown exponentially. The movement toward incarceration absent any attempt at offender reform has made the prison a place of uncompromising isolation and generally poor living conditions. In fact, prison conditions became so oppressive and violent as a result of this approach that the judiciary took notice. In *People v. Lovercamp*, the California Court of Appeals held that conditions of confinement could be used in certain cases to excuse escape. In this ruling, the court held that intolerable conditions, especially those that directly jeopardize the safety of an inmate, could serve as legal justification for flight. Other courts followed this example. A judicial allowance for escape suggests that the relationship between the prison and its inmates was changing, and not for the better.

As our nation has increasingly pursued a get-tough approach to crime, it has permitted offenders to mingle freely within our prisons with little consideration for their personal characteristics, the extent of their criminal activities or their amenability toward treatment. Based upon a biological approach, the current inmate population can and should be separated into two groups. The first group includes those young and relatively inexperienced inmates who have not yet made a full commitment to criminality. The second group consists of those inmates who are chronic, hardened and much more criminally experienced. This group has committed themselves to a criminal lifestyle and opposes treatment. By permitting these two populations to interact, the prison is allowing young, inexperienced and impressionable offenders to be unnecessarily influenced by those who are more criminally inclined. From a bio-penological perspective, social contagions are being transmitted within the prison and are having a negative impact upon the rehabilitation of amenable inmates. To address this problem it seems appropriate to separate those inmates that are spreading anti-social contagions from those that are not.

The Specialized Prison

In the previous chapter, we provided a rudimentary review for the historical foundation of prison specialization. This section continues that effort by providing additional information about these institutions. But before doing so it is necessary to recognize that early in our nation's history offender reform held a place of prominence. This is best reflected in the efforts of the Philadelphia Society for Alleviating the Miseries of Public Prisons (1790). This group, comprised entirely of interested citizens, sought to humanize the prison while protecting vulnerable inmates from those who were more hardened and violent. Members of this group eventually convinced officials of the Walnut Street Jail (America's first correctional institution) to separate young, inexperienced and less assertive inmates from those who held a more predatory and anti-social orientation. While this separation was based largely on gender, age and seriousness of offense, anecdotal evidence suggests that consideration was also given to each inmate's attitude toward authority and his/her perceived amenability toward reform. By separating members of these two groups, the opportunity was minimized for the hardened and predatory inmate to corrupt and victimize those who were malleable. Officials of the Elmira Reformatory (1869), an early prison that stressed ethics, religious instruction and vocational training, similarly acknowledged the existence of these two groups and recognized that achieving reform in such a mixed setting was improbable.

When we acknowledge the existence of these two groups, their separation becomes a reasonable means to prevent the spread of anti-social contagions. Anti-social contagions are those values, beliefs and behaviors that promote and perpetuate criminality. Once it is determined into which group an inmate belongs, he/she would then be housed with those similarly oriented. Nonamenable inmates would be housed with other nonamenable inmates. Likewise, amenable inmates would be housed together and would undergo educational, vocational and therapeutic programming. Since each amenable inmate would be an active and willing participant in his/her treatment program, a positive and supportive environment would develop. In essence, officials would be creating two unique penal environments. The first would be suited for those inmates who may best be described as violent, predatory and resistant to change. Officials would seek to control, contain and limit the ability of these inmates to victimize or corrupt others. The second environment would promote personal reform within an atmosphere where treatment would be buttressed by a supportive staff and a positive peer culture. The creation of this environment would differ from the culture of the contemporary prison in that it would:

- be free from negative peer pressure that promotes continued criminality and resistance to treatment,
- remove the stigma currently associated with participation in educational, vocational and therapeutic initiatives,
- create a safe and nurturing environment in which rehabilitation is supported and openly discussed by officials and inmates alike,
- result in the concentration of expertise and resources in a manner consistent with the intelligent and targeted delivery of treatment services, and
- promote mutual respect, accomplishment and a dedication to change among the inmate population.

Furthermore, specialization easily lends itself to indeterminate sentencing. Indeterminate sentencing stipulates a range of years during which an offender may be incarcerated. For example, an offender may be sentenced from 5-10 years, 10-20 years or any variation thereof. In the latter example, 10 is the minimum number of years that our inmate is to be imprisoned whereas 20 is the maximum number of years that he/she may be incarcerated. Our inmate will serve at least 10 years, but may serve 11, 12, 13, or perhaps the entire 20-year sentence. To this end, officials can refuse the early release of those inmates who are dangerous or who fail to make adequate progress toward rehabilitation. In essence, public safety becomes the primary determinant of release. While some portion of the inmate population would likely be confined up to the maximum limit of their sentence, it is this potential that provides an incentive for inmates to undergo treatment, pursue rehabilitation and to be serious in these endeavors. Provided that adequate progress is made, these inmates could earn early release at or near their minimum sentence term. As long as inmates have served at least their minimum sentence, are actively engaged in treatment and are displaying the signs of responsible behavior, release becomes a possibility. Indeterminate sentencing is valuable because it:

- recognizes that the promotion of public safety is the primary objective of the prison,
- promotes treatment, education and a pro-social orientation,
- replaces the traditional adversarial approach common in inmate-staff interaction with one that is more supportive and constructive,
- uses positive peer pressure to promote rehabilitation, and
- links early release to inmate rehabilitation.

This approach is based on the belief that incarceration is unpleasant, that most offenders already ascribe to conventional values, that inmates will openly and actively participate in treatment when it is promoted within a nurturing and supportive environment, and that early release is an incentive for change.

Currently, most jurisdictions operate under a fixed sentencing scheme where offenders are given a determinate sentence of 5, 10, perhaps even 20 years or any variation thereof. The only requirement for an inmate to obtain early release under this approach is that he/she refrains from engaging in conduct that threatens the safety and security of the institution. Provided that this requirement is met, an inmate will automatically be released after having served approximately half of his/her sentence. Therefore, an inmate that has been given a 5-year sentence can expect to be incarcerated for about 2.5 years. This is currently the preferred approach to sentencing since prisons are overcrowded and bed space is at a premium. Determinate sentencing moves inmates through the correctional system at an accelerated and predictable pace. It is based upon the flawed premise that if most inmates were required to serve longer portions of their sentence, as is a possibility under indeterminate sentencing options, the system would grind to a halt. The problem is that current approaches have effectively removed rehabilitation from release considerations. These approaches have also removed any incentive that may have previously existed for an inmate to engage in treatment or therapeutic activities. Currently, inmates are given early release with little or no consideration about their dangerousness or rehabilitation. Determinate sentencing is detrimental to public safety because it:

- fails to promote therapeutic initiatives,
- fails to promote a pro-social orientation or reinforce conventional values, and
- releases inmates without a consideration for their dangerousness or preparedness for full citizenship.

Prison specialization, when combined with indeterminate sentencing, creates an environment where the cessation of criminality, whether sought by way of punishment or treatment, becomes a system-wide objective. This approach impresses upon all inmates the importance of proper behavior and the need to take incarceration seriously. From a biological perspective, prison specialization and indeterminate sentencing would create an environment in which balance is achieved, growth is controlled and the spread of contagions is minimized. In essence, it would permit the prison to evolve into a more effective institution.

Conclusion

There are many social science perspectives attesting to the reformability of the contemporary offender. While current political posturing de-emphasizes rehabilitation, most inmates will eventually return to society. This observation alone should encourage penologists to seek innovative and creative ways to more effectively promote public safety. While a grassroots interest in treatment has been noted, little scholarship exists that describes how such interests are being translated into a conceptual framework.

Bio-penology suggests that current imprisonment initiatives will be unable to break the crime cycle until officials separate amenable and nonamenable inmates. The indiscriminate mixing of these two groups guarantees the ongoing contamination of young and inexperienced offenders. Furthermore, specialization requires officials to become more sensitive to the social health of the inmate population. By viewing the prison as a living organism and by recognizing that peer influence affects inmate behavior (both present and future), the spread of social contagions can be reduced.

The need remains, as it has for several decades, for the prison to return to an operational orientation that explicitly acts in the best interest of inmates and citizens. There is nothing to prevent the prison from actively pursuing both rehabilitation and punishment simultaneously. Pursuing both would permit the prison to more effectively achieve its potential. With recidivism rates at an all time high, the need for change is unmistakable. We must identify ways to minimize the negative and destructive influence of the prison's culture since to do so would facilitate the breaking of the crime cycle. The separation of amenable and nonamenable inmates appears to be a reasonable way to accomplish this task. Bio-penology requires that a decision be made about the future path of the prison and its relationship with the inmate population. For some inmates, simple confinement is the only form of correctional intervention that can be offered, while for others reform remains a possibility.

In the next chapter, you will be introduced to new ways of thinking about evolution, adaptation and change. You will also be asked to consider how these factors have affected and continue to affect the prison. An approach that uses a mixture of biology and physics to help explain observable phenomena is briefly introduced. Science has historically operated without established boundaries that separate what we now recognize as distinct disciplines. This traditional approach serves as the basis for contemporary efforts that seek to explain events in a more holistic manner. You will also be asked to consider how environment influences change. In particular, you will see that those changes that have occurred in the social and political realms have significantly altered the prison's ideology, objectives and operating procedures. While change is often viewed as necessary for the survival of a species, it can also have negative consequences. Viewed from this perspective, the prison has had little choice but to change. Yet these changes have had negative consequences for citizens and inmates, alike. So while the prison has indeed survived into the present day, it is of a fundamentally different genus that it was prior to the nineteen-eighties.

HIGHLIGHTS

- Penologists have an inherent responsibility to seek a greater understanding of those principles that govern the prison's operations.
- A prison's culture affects the post-release behaviors of its inmates. The source of this influence can be found in its pervasive and unique form of peer pressure.
- Inmate leaders are proficient at creating and perpetuating a culture of peer pressure that promotes opposition to all authority that is not inmate-based.
- Powerful and predatory inmates seek to create a prison culture that they can control, manipulate and exploit for personal gain.
- Presently, the inmate culture regulates all interactions between inmates, and between inmates and staff. However, it does not prohibit the predation of weaker inmates by those who are stronger and more criminally inclined.
- Social ecology suggests that environments share a number of characteristics in common with biological organisms. Among these similarities is the notion that communities can become sick and diseased.
- The prison is a socially isolated institution, suggesting that inmate leadership exerts an overwhelming degree of control over its culture.
- Cultural transmission suggests that a community's culture is transmitted to its residents through interaction and communication. One's length of residency becomes a factor in the transmission of a community's culture. The longer one's exposure to a particular community, the greater this effect.
- Peer influence is particularly pronounced within the prison where the peer-pool is limited and where contact is unavoidable, frequent and prolonged.
- A large percentage of the inmate population holds conventional values.
- Offenders engage in conventional behaviors a majority of the time. However, drift can occur causing an individual to move toward criminality. This drift may be caused by one's environment.

- An inmate may drift into and out of criminality provided that no commitment has been made to adopt criminality as a permanent lifestyle choice.

- It is a socially destructive practice to incarcerate offenders displaying a strong set of conventional values with those who do not.

- Stimulus-response suggests that behaviors that are deemed desirable by one's peers will result in acceptance and privilege while those that are deemed undesirable often result in exclusion and even retaliation. When applied to the penal setting, this perspective assumes even greater significance since young and impressionable offenders are in continual contact with those who are more criminally experienced. Since criminally experienced inmates control the prison, less experienced offenders have little choice but to adopt their ideology under threat of ostracism and violence.

- Those inmates who exercise the greatest amount of influence in the prison are those who are the most criminally inclined and violent.

- When a state of health and balance is achieved, organisms and institutions are able to effectively function; however, when a state of health and balance is not maintained, proper functioning is compromised.

- For most of the prison's history, punishment and rehabilitation have counterbalanced one another. Punishment ensures that the prison produces a deterrent effect while treatment humanizes the prison and promotes offender reform.

- The manner in which our prisons operate has a direct and lasting effect on the quality of life of virtually every citizen. In spite of its influence and its enormity, suggestions for improving the prison are noticeably absent from penal scholarship.

- As our nation has increasingly pursued a get-tough approach to crime, it has permitted offenders to mingle freely within our prisons with little consideration for their personal characteristics or criminal experiences.

- A judicial allowance for inmate escape suggests that the relationship between the prison and its inmates has changed, and not for the better.

- While early attempts at separating inmates were based on gender, age and seriousness of offense, anecdotal evidence suggests that a consideration was also given to each inmate's attitude toward authority and perceived reformability.

- Homeostasis is the ability of an organism or an institution to maintain a stable and healthy equilibrium.

- Growth is the tendency of an organism or an institution to increase in size. While growth is typically viewed as an indication of homeostasis, it does not always indicate health since unhealthy organisms and institutions also grow, and at times, growth itself is a consequence of sickness.

- If an institution can exist in a state of imbalance, then it stands to reason that it can similarly promote imbalance in others.

- Evolution refers to the ability of an organism to change in order to meet environmental challenges. Just as organisms can evolve, and in doing so often become more successful, so too can the prison.

- Bio-penology suggests that current imprisonment initiatives will be ineffective at breaking the crime cycle until officials separate amenable and nonamenable inmates.

- Bio-penology requires that a decision be made about the future of the prison and its relationship with the inmate population. For some inmates, simple confinement is the only form of correctional intervention that is prudent; for others, reform remains a possibility.

- When we acknowledge the existence of amenable and nonamenable inmates, their separation becomes a reasonable means to prevent the spread of anti-social contagions. Anti-social contagions are those values, beliefs and behaviors that promote and perpetuate criminality.

- By separating inmates based upon their amenability, the opportunity for the hardened and predatory inmate to corrupt and victimize those who are more malleable is minimized.

- Prison specialization easily lends itself to indeterminate sentencing.

- When operating under indeterminate sentencing, a prison's officials can refuse the early release of those inmates who are dangerous or who are failing to make adequate progress toward rehabilitation.

- Determinate sentencing effectively removes any incentive that may have previously existed for an inmate to engage in treatment or therapeutic activities. Currently, inmates are given early release with little or no consideration about their dangerousness or progress toward rehabilitation.

QUESTIONS

1). What value is there in considering prison operations from a biological perspective? What similarities and differences exist between living organisms and the prison? Explain your responses and be as descriptive as possible.

2). What characteristics of the inmate culture make it especially influential? Explain.

3). Describe the potential effect of cultural transmission on the post release behaviors of an inmate that has been incarcerated for a prolonged period of time (in excess of ten years)?

4). In your opinion, do most inmates ascribe to conventional values and if so, how do you explain "drift"?

5). Do the objectives of rehabilitation and punishment counterbalance each other? What are the effects of pursuing one of these objectives more aggressively than the other? Explain.

6). Currently, inmates are separated based upon age and gender. Should they also be separated based upon demeanor toward authority and treatment? Explain. What effect, if any, would such an approach have on recidivism rates?

CHAPTER THREE
Evolutionary Science

Change can save an institution
from extinction or doom it to decline.

The ideas contained within this chapter are based upon insights obtained from evolutionary science. As a subfield of biology, evolutionary scientists study changes that occur in all living organisms. We now know that over time, all change can be thought of as having either a positive or negative effect. Positive changes permit a species to more effectively adapt to its environment, increasing survivability. Negative changes place a species at a disadvantage and may force it into decline and even extinction. It is intuitive then that only those species that develop in a positive fashion will survive over prolonged periods of time.

Perhaps the evolutionary scientists best known to the contemporary layman is Charles Darwin, author of *On the Origin of Species* (1859). Darwin wrote about natural selection, genetic mutations, competition and environmental stressors. His efforts brought evolution to the forefront of scientific discussion. And while we should recognize Darwin's many contributions to this field, the basis for evolutionary science can be traced back to the Greek and Roman eras. For example, Lucretius wrote *On the Nature of Things* (50 BC) which presented a discourse on biology, reproduction and physics. Aristotle is also credited with providing a basis for this field of inquiry. Others who have contributed to its more recent development include Pierre Louis Maupertuis who authored *Derivation of the Laws of Motion and Equilibrium from a Metaphysical Principle* (1746), William Paley in *Natural Theology or Evidences of the Existence and Attributes of the Deity* (1802), and Jean-Baptiste Lamarck with his transmutation theory (a predecessor of Darwin's theory of natural selection) (1809). While other scholars have helped shape our views, these scientists are among the most celebrated. As a point of interest, many early scientists often blended biology with physics, failing to draw a distinction between the two. Referred to as natural philosophy, this unique approach predates the creation of separate scientific disciplines and the rigid use of systematic, quantitative and replicable procedures. Natural philosophy serves as a conceptual basis for all contemporary efforts that seek to further our knowledge by crossing disciplinary boundaries.

Change, Evolution and Adaptation

For the purposes of this chapter, the word change refers generically to both evolution and adaptation in their single and collective capacities. More specifically, the term evolution as used hereafter refers to changes that occur at the genetic level. This type of change is beyond the control of a species. These changes include the development of camouflage, physical defense mechanisms and unique corporeal features that permit a species to more fully exploit its environment. For example, the chameleon can assume the colors of its habitat making it virtually invisible to predators and prey. Likewise, the giraffe's long neck allows it to obtain food beyond the reach of other savanna herbivores. Conversely, the term adaptation, as we use it, refers to behavioral changes that include the southward migration of waterfowl during the winter months as well as the famous Japanese snow monkeys that escape frigid mountain temperatures by soaking in natural hot springs! Behavioral change is undertaken in a deliberate and calculated manner. Each of these examples, as you can clearly see, showcases behaviors that are intended to increase survivability. When positive change occurs (whether genetic or behavioral):

- a species becomes more effective in dealing with environmental challenges,
- it becomes increasingly easier for a species to obtain needed resources, and
- a greater number of offspring are produced and survive to maturity.

Once a positive change or a succession of positive changes have occurred, a species will find that its forward momentum (borrowing imagery from physics) will enable it to obtain needed resources with increasing ease. This increased level of success may permit it to eventually dominate its niche or environment. As the species reproduces in greater numbers, population growth occurs. And while growth is routinely used to measure the overall success of a species, it often results in increased competition and, at some point, widespread disease and death. This suggests that uncontrolled growth can ultimately have devastating consequences. When negative change occurs (whether genetic or behavioral):

- a species becomes less adept at dealing with environmental challenges,
- it becomes increasingly more difficult for the species to obtain food and shelter, and
- fewer offspring are produced and/or survive to maturity.

Negative change brings with it challenges that will, over time, adversely affect a species' survivability. Once a state of decline has begun, a species' momentum (again, borrowing imagery from physics) becomes exponentially more difficult but not impossible to overcome. For example, as a species begins to encounter difficulty, two possibilities exist. First, some random genetic mutation(s) may occur that delivers it from a state of decline. Or a species may adopt behaviors that prove beneficial for its long-term survival. Remember the snow monkeys that escape frigid winter temperatures by soaking in natural hot springs? Their behavior, even though they are naturally fearful of water and heat, is deliberately undertaken to ensure that they survive a harsh, deadly environment. Therefore, both happenstance as well as deliberate action may have a dramatic effect on a species' survivability. Regardless of whether or not change improves the chances for survival, evolutionary science acknowledges that it will continue unabated for as long as a species exists.

Whether positively or negatively oriented, a species is forever locked in a cycle whereby change is either undertaken in an accidental, haphazard and random manner as is illustrated by genetic mutation or is the result of environmental stressors that bring about behavior modification. Regardless of the source of change or a species' degree of success, the ultimate outcome is usually the same. This outcome will either be an overall reduction in the number of a species' members that results from an inability to compete successfully (via negative change) or a reduction in membership that results from a species being so successful (via positive change) that it must experience a culling event (a temporary reduction in membership). It is during a culling event that a species' numbers are reduced until equilibrium is again obtained. Equilibrium, in this sense, is determined by the number of a species' members that can be supported by an environment over prolonged periods of time. It is important to understand that growth has its limits. Nature will only permit a species to be successful up to a certain point. If a species ventures beyond that point, growth will cease and membership will decline usually due to diminishing resources, disease or increased predation. Lemmings, rodents and certain deer routinely experience these events. The point that we wish to make is that change can either occur in a random and uncontrolled fashion or it can be a conscience and deliberate choice. Furthermore, change can resurrect an unsuccessful species, saving it from extinction, or it may doom an otherwise successful species to decline. Regardless, change tends to have a detrimental effect for those members of a species that are weak or marginalized. Change often prevents some portion of a population from reproducing or participating fully in communal affairs. The phrase "survival of the fittest" was specifically coined to express this phenomenon in a more genteel fashion.

Evolutionary Science and the Prison

One axiom of evolutionary science is that if change is too radical or if it occurs too abruptly, it will almost certainly have devastating consequences. This observation, while being applicable to the natural realm, is also relevant to the social realm. Throughout this book you will be introduced to subtle and overt changes that have affected, and continue to affect, the prison. While this information spans the entire history of our correctional system, of particular interest are those changes that have occurred during the latter half of the twentieth century. It is these changes that have ultimately shaped the ideology and operations of the modern prison. These changes are of three varieties. The first can be thought of as being environmental in nature. These include changes that have occurred within our social and political spheres. An appropriate example includes a growing level of conservatism that has served as a precursor for the remaining two varieties. The second pertains to those changes that have been forced upon the prison. An example of this second variety includes huge increases in our inmate populations (beginning in about 1980) and the subsequent overcrowding of our correctional facilities. The third and final variety includes those changes that are undertaken by prison officials in a calculated and deliberate manner. These changes include the prison's willful abandonment of treatment. To elucidate the differences between these varieties of change, consider that those that were environmental in nature included:

- an increasingly conservative political climate that culminated in the election of Ronald Reagan. This conservative ideology was exhibited in Reagan's no-nonsense approach when dealing with issues pertaining to the nation's offenders,

- legislation, enforcement and judicial activities and decisions that increasingly embraced a punitive ideology,
- a "nothing works" perspective that sought to punish offenders without regard for treatment, education or rehabilitation, and
- a financial orientation that sought drastic reductions in government spending by eliminating all non-essential services.

These environmental changes placed the prison under a great deal of strain. The primary source for this strain was a growing level of conservatism that viewed the offender in a hostile manner. This resulted in a call for increasingly harsh punishments with the added demand for efficiency through the elimination of treatment programs. To justify this approach, advocates suggested that harsh punishments (as measured in lengthier terms of incarceration), when delivered in an institution devoid of therapeutic initiatives, would produce a deterrent effect - thereby lowering crime rates. It stood to reason that no one in his/her right mind would commit a crime knowing that such a fate might await. As the social and political environments began to change, prisons (which are comparable to any biological species) began to experience internal changes. These changes can be compared to those genetic changes over which a species has no control. Those "genetic" changes that began to occur within the prison included:

- an increase in the number of offenders committed to its care and custody,
- an increase in the average term of incarceration,
- a space shortage, causing many prisons to operate at 200%-300% capacity, and
- a growing relationship with the private sector to build and operate facilities to house inmate overflow.

In essence, not only were the social and political environments changing, but significant changes were also occurring within the prison itself. While the prison had no control over these changes, it was expected to adjust quickly, expand as necessary and to operate in a manner that was consistent with those expectations being established by legislators. If you doubt the lack of control that the prison had over just one of these factors, let's say the number of offenders being committed to its care and custody, imagine what would have transpired had an administrator posted a "no vacancy" sign on the front door of his/her facility. These changes had a collective influence on the ideology and operational practices of the prison. And while there is anecdotal evidence to suggest that not all correctional officials were ready to embrace this new conservatism, the prison was nonetheless on the cusp of an evolutionary event.

As environmental and "genetic" factors exerted their collective influence over the prison, correctional officials deliberately:

- aligned themselves with those politicians that controlled state budgets,
- adopted a fiscal conservatism that reduced or eliminated all non-essential activities or programs including those pertaining to treatment,
- refused to accept any responsibility for the future behaviors of ex-inmates,
- downplayed the importance of recidivism rates as a measure of correctional performance,
- created new performance measures that were based upon internal attributes, and
- hired staff with little regard for their qualifications and commitment to the corrections field.

As you can see, these behavioral changes were designed to ingratiate prison officials to those politicians that were controlling state budgets. By aligning themselves with political leadership, prison authorities were able to lobby for increased funding. This approach proved quite effective. In fact, financial support for prison expansion far outpaced similar support for higher education and even healthcare. Nonetheless, prison officials increasingly found it difficult to house and support growing inmate populations. To meet ongoing budgetary shortfalls and in an attempt to stay aligned with the politically elite, prison officials reduced and eliminated most non-essential programs. Not only did these actions meet with the satisfaction of a conservative powerbase, but it liberated funds to help finance further expansion. This had three significant consequences. First, by cutting treatment, the prison was placed in a position by which it had to downplay the importance of rehabilitation. Secondly, prison officials had to disavow any responsibility for the future criminal activities of its ex-inmates. It stood to reason that since prisons were no longer places that were responsible for rehabilitating offenders, then crimes committed by ex-inmates could no longer be visited upon the correctional system. In essence, officials had now undertaken a radical departure from those traditional ideologies that had long driven the prison's operations. By freeing itself from the expectations associated with rehabilitation, and by distancing itself from any responsibility for breaking the crime cycle, the prison had fundamentally altered its nature. It is interesting to note that the prison's official did this freely, with full intent, and with the knowledge and blessings of the nation's political leadership. And finally, since efficiency was now paramount, a less qualified staff was hired. Remember, a prison that seeks to warehouse inmates requires a much different type of employee than does a prison that values treatment, rehabilitation and education.

Once freed from traditional expectations and constraints, prison officials had to develop a new way to measure success. No longer would recidivism rates be used to determine how effective the prison was at promoting public safety, instead, new standards of success would have to be created. These new standards, in an attempt to give officials more control over their public image, would be related to internal attributes. After all, measures of internal attributes could be easily manipulated to give the impression of success. By replacing recidivism (which is an external and transparent measure) with internal measures often pertaining to efficiency and profit, and by claiming that these newer measures were legitimate reflections of the prison's social value, officials had created the foundation for the largest human warehousing experiment ever undertaken. The prison had entered an evolutionary stage where its actions would increasingly be governed by self-interests, expansion and a desire for profit.

The Evolved Prison

The prison that began to emerge during the 1980s, while physically resembling its predecessor is a much different species indeed. The contemporary prison is largely driven by self-interest and an increasing desire to operate outside traditional parameters. In other words, prisons of today are primarily concerned with acquiring a greater annual proportion of each state's budget, freeing themselves from treatment ideologies, downplaying the significance of recidivism rates and promoting a public image of efficiency. There is no doubt that the business model, which seeks continual expansion, is being applied to the contemporary prison. When financial issues shape correctional discourse and a fiscal conservativism determines the ideology and nature of the prison's actions, the public's long-term safety becomes a secondary concern. Consider if you will that the modern prison is characterized by:

- continual growth (and the expressed desire thereof),
- a dismissal of any and all interest in, or responsibility for, the future actions of ex-inmates,
- an almost complete cessation of references to education, treatment, rehabilitation and recidivism within departmental communiqués,
- a systemic ignorance of traditional penal objectives,
- a lowering of standards as they pertain to employment and training, and
- its attempt to create a positive public image while simultaneously shielding its actions from scrutiny and oversight.

These characteristics are certainly not flattering but they are accurate. And while the prison has long been plagued by inhumane treatment, the objectification of inmates, and a desire to operate cheaply, these characteristics have never been more pronounced. While the prison no longer practices brutal forms of punishment, the observation can be made that incarceration is now a brutal form of punishment in and of itself. The prison's actions now affect such a large percentage of our population that its operations must be placed within its proper context. As such, we should view the sheer size of the inmate population, their overall treatment, and the ramifications for discarding ideologies pertaining to treatment and rehabilitation as a public health issue. Or stated a bit differently, if inmates are being deprived of an opportunity to better themselves during their terms of incarceration, then it stands to reason that most will be adversely affected by the experience. This situation places citizens unfairly in harm's way. An untold number of crimes are perpetrated upon citizens each year by ex-inmates that have not been prepared to assume productive positions in society. This suggests that the prison will go to virtually any length (i.e. withholding treatment) as a way to passively ensure a constant and growing need for its service.

So you see, whether we are talking about a particular species whose survival is being threatened or an institution that is confronting changes in the social and political spheres, environment plays a key role in determining the nature and purpose of behavior. While the prison has had to confront drastic environmental changes, and while it was increasingly forced to operate in an overcrowded manner, it was not forced to jettison its interest in treatment or its pursuit of rehabilitation. Nor was the prison forced to abandon recidivism as the ultimate measure for determining its level of effectiveness at promoting public safety. While change is inevitable, officials deliberately adopted a set of behaviors that sent the prison down an evolutionary path whereby its actions were no longer undertaken to promote the long-term health and well being of the inmate or society, but were instead self-serving. In essence, just like any wild beast, self-preservation and growth have become the prison's primary concerns.

Conclusion

Our ability to view phenomena from differing perspectives has long been recognized as an effective mechanism to solve problems and to increase our understanding of the natural and social realms. By considering the prison from the perspective of evolutionary science, we gain insight into its operations and those factors that have governed its own evolutionary trajectory. Among these early factors was a growing level of conservatism which increasingly called for harsher punishments and government efficiency. These factors, in turn, led to changes within the prison. These changes can be thought of as being genetic or behavioral in nature. Genetic changes are those that were forced upon the prison and were beyond its control. A good example of a genetic change was the swelling of inmate populations. These populations quickly doubled and tripled, leaving prisons severely overcrowded. The prison had no choice but to accommodate these huge increases. Behavioral changes were those that the prison undertook in a deliberate manner. Among these were the jettisoning of treatment ideologies and the abandonment of recidivism rates as the universally recognized measure for gauging the prison's ability to promote public safety.

There is little doubt that the prison has changed considerably in the past few decades. It has become a large industrial undertaking that seeks to process and warehouse huge numbers of people in an increasingly efficient manner. And while it had little initial control over its growth, it has nonetheless freely adopted an operational perspective that is an antithesis of its original purpose. It essence, by discarding a treatment ideology, the prison's administrators have removed the only operational objective that specifically prevents offender objectification. Once a person or an entire group of people are objectified, they can easily be exploited, manipulated and discarded at will. The very purpose of a treatment ideology was to ensure that the prison would measure its success not by a growing need for its services but by a decreasing need for those services. This is the only proper way to measure the prison's effectiveness. When we look at it this way, the prison hasn't evolved over the past 50 years, it has de-evolved. In doing so, its actions and objectives have become more primitive in nature.

In the next chapter, we will make the transition from a biological perspective to one that compares particles to prisoners. It is within this exploration that peer influence, the Hawthorne Effect and energy are considered. Furthermore, it is argued that like particles, inmates are either positively or negatively oriented. Those inmates with a positive orientation will be likened to protons and those with a negative orientation will be compared to electrons. It is surmised that when opposite charges or orientations are present within a system, energy and peer influence tend to flow in one direction - from the negative toward the positive state. If this is indeed the case, then an insulator must be employed to protect amenable inmates from the corrupting influence of those who oppose treatment initiatives.

HIGHLIGHTS

- As a subfield of biology, evolutionary science considers those changes that occur in all living organisms.
- Changes may be genetic or behavioral in nature.
- Over time, all species change in either positive or negative ways.
- Positive change permits a species to more effectively adapt to its environment, helping ensure survivability.
- Negative change places a species at a disadvantage and may force it into decline or extinction.
- Perhaps the best known evolutionist is Charles Darwin, author of *On the Origin of Species* (1859).
- Because of Darwin's efforts, evolution was brought to the forefront of scientific discussion.
- The basis for evolutionary science can be traced to the Greek and Roman eras.
- Many early scientists blended biology and physics, failing to draw a clear distinction between the two. Referred to as natural philosophy, this unique approach predates the creation of separate academic disciplines and the use of systematic, quantitative and replicable procedures.
- The term evolution, as we use it, refers to changes that occur at the genetic level and are beyond the control of a species. These changes include the development of camouflage, physical defense mechanisms and unique corporeal features that permit a species to more fully exploit its environment.
- Genetic change is beyond the control of a species.
- The term adaptation, as we use it, refers to behavioral changes that include the southward migration of waterfowl during the winter months, as well as the famous Japanese snow monkeys that escape frigid mountain temperatures by soaking in natural hot springs.

- Behavioral change is undertaken deliberately.

- There are three varieties of change that have affected the prison. The first was environmental, occurring in the social and political spheres. The second variety was beyond the prison's control and is therefore, comparable to genetic changes. Since the third variety was deliberately undertaken, they are comparable to those behavioral changes that occur in the natural realm.

- Once a positive change has occurred, a species will find it increasingly easier to obtain needed resources.

- Uncontrolled growth can ultimately have devastating consequences.

- Growth has its limits. Nature only permits a species to be successful up to a certain point. If a species ventures beyond that point, growth ceases and membership declines.

- Negative change brings with it challenges that will, over time, adversely affect a species' survivability.

- Evolutionary science acknowledges that regardless of whether or not change improves survivability, it will continue unabated for as long as a species exists.

- Whether positively or negatively oriented, change is undertaken in either an accidental, haphazard and random manner, as is illustrated by genetic mutation, or is the result of environmental stressors that bring about modifications to behavior.

- Regardless of the source of change or a species' degree of success, the outcome will always be the same - an eventual reduction in the number of a species' members either due to its inability to compete, or because it has been so successful that it must experience a culling event.

- A culling event is when a species' numbers are reduced (due to diminishing resources, disease, competition or predation) until equilibrium is again obtained.

- Equilibrium is determined by the number of a species' members that can be supported by an environment over prolonged periods of time.

- Change can resurrect an unsuccessful species, saving it from extinction or it may doom an otherwise successful species to decline.
- Whether change is positively or negatively oriented, its immediate consequences are always detrimental to those members who are weak or marginalized.
- One axiom of evolutionary science is that if change is too radical or it if occurs too abruptly it will almost certainly have devastating consequences.
- During the final decades of the twentieth century, growing social and political conservatism resulted in a demand for efficient prison operations, increasingly harsh penalties and the elimination of treatment programs.
- A prison that warehouses inmates requires a different type of employee than does a prison that values treatment, rehabilitation and education.
- As the social and political environments began to change, the prison (comparable to any biological species) changed in order to survive.

QUESTIONS

1). Many early scientists blended biology and physics, failing to draw a clear distinction between the two. Is there an advantage to such an approach? Does this approach offer any promise for increasing our understanding of natural phenomena? Does it offer promise for increasing our understanding of social phenomena? Explain.

2). What are the primary differences between evolution and adaptation? In addition to those examples already given, can you think of other examples that illustrate each within the natural realm? Can you think of any examples that pertain to the social realm? Has the prison evolved or de-evolved over the past few decades? Provide evidence to support your position.

3). We noted that population growth is often considered a measure of a species' success. Does growth have its limits? Explain. Can it result in negative consequences? Explain. What implications does this have for the prison? Explain.

4). How accurate is the statement, "change can resurrect an unsuccessful species, saving it from extinction or it may doom an otherwise successful species to decline"? Explain.

5). How accurate is the statement, "if change is too radical or if it occurs too abruptly, it will almost certainly have devastating consequences"? Explain. What implications does this have for the prison? Explain.

6). What are the differences between environmental, genetic and behavioral changes as they relate to the prison?

7). What were the environmental conditions that ultimately caused changes to occur within the prison? Were these conditions largely social or political in nature? Explain.

8). In your opinion, have the changes that have occurred to the prison during the past few decades had positive or negative consequences for the inmate? Have these changes had positive or negative consequences for public safety? Explain.

9). What is meant by the phrase, "A prison that seeks to warehouse inmates requires a much different type of employee than does a prison that values treatment, rehabilitation and education"? Explain.

CHAPTER FOUR
Sub-atomic Particles and Prisoners

If energy and peer influence are comparable, and if particles and prisoners are similar, then it is the negatively charged inmate that affects those with a positive orientation.

As you are certainly aware of by now, we are interested in the natural sciences and how they may be applied to penology. This interest has required us to become acquainted with the works of many twentieth century scientists. As we have become familiar with these individuals and their thoughts, we have discovered many commonalities that exist between the natural and the social realms. We now believe that the scientific lines separating these seemingly divergent domains are little more than arbitrary constructs. In reality, overlap exists between all academic fields with none being able to claim a monopoly on information or how it may be used to improve the human condition. All things are interconnected. The challenge for the modern scientist is to discover those connections that exist between the natural and social worlds. If done correctly, this endeavor promises to enhance our understanding of human experiences, choices and behaviors. The great physicist Albert Einstein spent a large portion of his life attempting to explain both the atomic and celestial realms. He insisted that natural events are the direct and predictable result of universal laws. This belief has similarly led us to apply natural laws to the social world in an attempt to increase our understanding of human and institutional behavior. Since Dr. Einstein was a physicist and since physics is the most fundamental of all sciences, we decided to consider it further.

Critical to the approach taken herein is the unification of scientific disciplines. Einstein himself helped establish the Olympian Academy which sought knowledge from a variety of social, philosophical and scientific sources. The activities of this and similar groups have foreshadowed recent attempts to eliminate the barriers that separate the sciences. For example, the current buzzword in academia is interdisciplinarity. This term refers to combining two or more academic disciplines to obtain insight into a particular area of inquiry. This approach gives researchers a license to cross traditional boundaries as a means to enhance exploration and increase the likelihood for discovery. Within the context of this book, biological principles (as was done in the previous chapter) and physics (as is the case in this and subsequent chapters) are used to acquire insight into prison operations and their effect on recidivism, offender rehabilitation and ultimately, public safety. As we have acquainted ourselves with physics, we have also become aware that physicists have long insisted that a connection exists between all fields. Lee Smolin, Hans Bethe, Freeman Dyson, and Jerome Rothstein, each an acclaimed physicist, have asserted that all serious efforts to advance knowledge must be rooted in an interdisciplinary approach. In fact, physicists are increasingly using their unique insights to explain human behavior. Through our exploration of the natural sciences, we have discovered that the number of similarities and connections existing between physics and penology are numerous and might easily serve as the basis for many books.

Before continuing, it is necessary that you understand that we are not physicists nor do we wish to present ourselves as such. Instead, we are social scientists whose current efforts are undertaken for three specific reasons that include a desire to:

- promote creative and innovative thinking as a means to improve the prison,
- convince our readers that commonalities exist between seemingly divergent fields, and
- encourage cooperation across disciplines by showing that these incursions can be fun, inventive and ultimately informative.

It is also important, in an attempt to avoid confusion, to define a few terms. The term socio-physics refers to an interdisciplinary approach that blends the social and physical sciences as a way to increase our understanding of the prison and its impact on criminality. We also occasionally use the term socio-physicists to refer to those scientists who see a value in applying physics to the study of human behavior. And finally, the term particle refers to protons and electrons (each of which will be defined shortly) while the term atom refers to these particles as well as the nuclei around which they accrue.

In the Realm of the Atom

For those of you unfamiliar with physics, it may appear a bit peculiar to compare particles to prisoners. Yet physicists and penologists engage in similar activities. For example, at their most basic level, scientists in both fields practice environmental manipulation. While manipulation in physics usually occurs in a laboratory, manipulation of the prison's environment is also common. In fact, decisions that range from an institution's paint scheme to the presence of its security personnel are intended to affect inmate behavior. And while physicists study everything from particles to the vast expanse of the universe, for the socio-physicist, inmates serve as our particles while the prison is comparable to the cosmos.

An interdisciplinary approach that uses a natural sciences' perspective may increase our understanding of how the prison affects an offender's post release behavior. Central to the natural sciences is a consideration of environment and its impact on biological organisms and systems. An understanding of environment and its effects on behavior is necessary since nearly 650,000 inmates are released from our prisons each year, amounting to about 1,800 each day. The post release behavior of these offenders will largely determine crime rates. This makes rehabilitation an important consideration. Because of the expense associated with supporting our nation's inmate population, officials have reduced or eliminated most non-essential services. Non-essential services include those programs that are not absolutely necessary from an operational viewpoint. Strictly speaking, these are activities that are ancillary to the safe and orderly operation of a facility. Included among these are most treatment programs. Reductions of this nature, while perhaps necessary from a budgetary perspective, prove unpopular among Americans. Nearly 90% of our citizens support the pursuit of offender rehabilitation. Nonetheless, jurisdictions find it increasingly difficult to fund therapeutic programs. With the annual cost of operating America's correctional system exceeding $60 billion a year, a great deal of interest exists in identifying approaches that promise to enhance the effectiveness of correctional intervention.

Pertinent to socio-physics is the work of Werner Heisenberg (1901-1976). Heisenberg, a German theoretical physicist, made substantial contributions to the field of quantum mechanics. Quantum mechanics is a specialized branch of physics that studies the relationship between energy and matter at the atomic level. Heisenberg developed what is popularly known as the Heisenberg Uncertainty Principle. For our purpose, this principle consists of two parts. The first deals with a physicist's inability to know both the location and momentum of a particle. It stipulates that an observer can never know both properties simultaneously. In normal situations, a physicist can determine a particle's location or its momentum, but never both. If physicists were able to ascertain both properties simultaneously, more would be known about particle behavior. Heisenberg's work is especially relevant to the penal setting since it would similarly prove beneficial for penologists to ascertain an offender's location (referring to his/her level of experience which ranges from first-time to habitual offender) and momentum (which relates to the speed at which this experience is being obtained). This information could then be used to make a determination about an offender's amenability, treatment options and their appropriate level of intensity, and an overall course of action that might yield the best probability for offender reform.

The second component of this Principle suggests that observation itself changes the behavior of atomic particles. This portion of the Heisenberg Uncertainty Principle (often referred to as the Heisenberg Effect) is illustrated in the question, "If a tree falls in a forest and no one is around to hear it, does it make a sound?" While the object in this example is a tree and not a particle, it serves a similar purpose. Many physicists, especially those involved in the early development of quantum mechanics, would argue that without an observer, the tree may have acted differently, perhaps failing to produce the telltale cracking and popping sounds associated with falling timber. Philosopher George Berkeley is the first scholar known to have raised this question (1734). Other versions of this query have appeared in popular texts including Michio Kaku and Jennifer Thompson's *Beyond Einstein* (1987) and Charles Mann and George Twiss' *Physics* (1910). The act of observation appears especially pertinent to determining behavior. If observation can affect particle behavior then it is reasonable to assume that it also affects human behavior. Thus, it can be manipulated to produce positive results. The prison is specifically designed to maximize opportunities for surveillance and can therefore, if used properly, help shape the current and future behaviors of its inmate population.

Physicists have also observed that strong relationships tend to develop among particles within the same system. Referred to as quantum entanglement (a term coined by physicist Erwin Schrodinger), the relationship between these particles can become so strong that it is impossible to describe one of these linked particles without describing the others. These particles become so similar in behavior that for all intents and purposes their actions are in perfect synchrony and they become one object even though they remain separate. The destinies of these particles stay inextricably and instantaneously connected, defying distance itself. In fact, Einstein (speaking in German) called this "spukhafte fernwirkung" which means "spooky action at a distance". While the causes of entanglement remain unknown, it nonetheless reveals the powerful effects that relationships can have on behavior. Now imagine for a moment that these particles are prisoners who, upon associating with one another, become similarly linked. Once entangled, an inmate's current and future behaviors may be somewhat dependent on the actions, values and beliefs of his/her associates. If this is the case, the question becomes "to whom do we want our amenable inmates to be linked?" The answer to this question is obvious - we should strive to have our amenable inmate population linked to those individuals who promote a pro-social orientation. Again, if associations can affect particle behavior, then it is reasonable to assume that they can also affect human behavior and can therefore be manipulated to produce positive results.

Socio-Physics: The Blending of Two Sciences

While the Heisenberg Effect pertains specifically to physics, a similar effect also exists within the social sciences. Perhaps the most famous sociological study ever conducted in the United States showcasing this effect was undertaken (1924-1932) at the Hawthorne Works Factory located near Chicago, Illinois. Since the completion of this study, the name Hawthorne has become synonymous with behavioral changes resulting from observation, environmental manipulation and increased expectations. While the findings of this study are voluminous, suffice it to say that the owners of Hawthorne wanted to improve employee productivity. To this end, they made changes in lighting, implemented employee breaks and provided workers with gratis meals. All of these modifications were made with the expectation that employees would subsequently become more productive. Ultimately, productivity did increase leading researchers to conclude that employees altered their behaviors to coincide with these changes. In essence, observation, environmental manipulation and increased expectations produced a positive result with regard to employee behavior.

While changes were largely perceived by the workforce as being favorable, a small group of employees came to resent and openly oppose them. Talking, horseplay, insubordination, hostility and poor productivity became the hallmark characteristics of this group. Members of this group created their own code of conduct with anecdotal evidence suggesting that they were attempting to promote a culture of opposition to these changes and wished to have a similar attitude adopted factory-wide. This group effectively sought to create a hostile and oppositional environment to thwart the efforts of supervisors and researchers, alike. However, intervention was undertaken by the factory's owners to minimize and when appropriate eliminate this group's effects upon the morale of the other employees. Thus, two employee groups emerged, those who were cooperative and amenable toward change and those who were resistant and nonamenable. For our purpose, the significance of this study is threefold:

- first, positive changes in attitude and behavior were brought about by observation, environmental manipulation and increased expectation,
- secondly, changes created a renewed sense of pride, accomplishment and ultimately improved productivity, and
- two groups emerged - those who were oriented toward change and those who were change-resistant.

The Uncertainty Principle and the Heisenberg/Hawthorne Effects are especially relevant to our consideration. For example, while it remains impossible for physicists to simultaneously know both the location and momentum of an individual particle, the location and momentum of an individual offender is attainable. In fact, socio-physicists are aware of this information's value and can ascertain an offender's location and momentum in a simultaneous fashion through interviews, observations and a review of one's criminal record. While this information is easily obtainable, it is not widely used to determine an offender's amenability. This has, in turn, hindered existing treatment initiatives. Yet, for the socio-physicist, location is identical to criminal experience. An assessment of one's location provides insight into the extent to which an offender has matured within the criminal lifestyle. Similarly, an assessment of one's momentum provides insight into his/her attitude about criminality and correctional intervention. Since each of these factors is closely associated with attitude, an inmate can be described as being positively or negatively oriented. This determination provides insight into the probable success of therapeutic intervention and reveals which forms of intervention may be the most effective. A positive orientation reflects an attitude favorable toward treatment whereas a negative orientation signifies an oppositional attitude. If an offender has a great deal of criminal experience and is negatively oriented, it may be difficult or even impossible to slow or halt criminality through treatment, but if it is determined that an offender is in the early stages of his/her criminal career and is positively oriented, then intensive treatment delivered in a supportive and nurturing environment could end an otherwise extensive career. We must be fully aware that observation, environmental manipulation and increased expectations can and do have a significant effect on behavior. One's environment and one's associates are instrumental in promoting either a pro-social and positive orientation or an orientation that is less constructive. From this point onward, energy and peer influence will be considered equivalent with the only difference being the realm in which each exists. This equivalency will become more important within the next few pages.

Collectively, the Heisenberg Principle and the Hawthorne Experiment suggest that similarities exist between the atomic and social realms and subsequently, between the particle and prisoner. These similarities are as follows:

- an observer-effect is present in both realms - in the atomic realm it is referred to as the Heisenberg Effect, whereas in the social realm it is referred to as the Hawthorne Effect,
- while observation affects particle behavior it similarly affects the behaviors of people,
- a majority of those individuals placed under observation react in a positive manner while a minority adopt an oppositional approach,
- mechanisms can be implemented to minimize and even eliminate the adverse effects associated with negative peer pressure and a culture of opposition,
- the probability that positive changes will occur in behavior increase when observation is combined with environmental modification and increased expectation,
- various behaviors within the atomic realm can be attributed to particle-entanglement whereas in the social setting various behaviors can be attributed to peer-entanglement,
- in the atomic realm, particles carry positive or negative charges, while in the social realm humans can be visualized as being similarly oriented,
- those inmates who are of a positive orientation can be visualized as being good candidates for change, whereas those who are negatively oriented, because of their oppositional attitude, are poor candidates for change,
- when opposite charges or orientations are present within a system (be it in the atomic or penal realm), energy and peer influence tend to flow in one direction - from the negative toward a positive state, and
- if energy and peer influence flow from a negative to a positive state, then positively oriented inmates should be housed separately from those of a negative orientation as a means to reduce and even eliminate destructive influences.

For the purpose of this effort, we shall liken the prison to the nucleus of an atom. The nucleus serves as the unifying force around which particles congregate; the prison serves a similar function by making congregation and interaction among inmates (our particles) possible. The proton, since it carries a positive charge, is comparable to those inmates who have not fully committed themselves to a criminal lifestyle and are amenable toward treatment. Since the electron carries a negative charge, it can be compared (because it is a negative force) to those inmates who embrace criminality and disavow therapeutic intervention. Furthermore, as previously stated, we consider energy and peer influence to have similar properties and to be functional equivalents. As such, the flow of energy among particles is always from a negative toward a positive state. If energy and peer influence are comparable, and if particles and prisoners are similar, then it is the negatively oriented inmate who influences those of a positive orientation. At present, the prison (because it is a negative environment and since its officials have permitted a culture of opposition to flourish) tends to have a corruptive influence, thereby adversely affecting the orientation and criminal momentum of many amenable offenders.

Prisoners Behaving Like Particles?

It has long been observed that offenders and non-offenders tend to hold similar values, with offenders engaging in conventional behaviors a majority of the time. Pro-social values are often evident in the guilt that offenders experience after they have committed a crime. Yet, correctional practitioners and penologists are aware that pro-social values can deteriorate through exposure to a negatively charged environment. If pro-social values can be weakened by contact with a negative environment, then it is reasonable to assume that they can also be strengthened through exposure to positive and pro-social environments.

It has similarly been noted that experienced and violent inmates have created a prison culture that rejects all authority that is not inmate based. In addition to opposing correctional efforts, this culture requires less experienced inmates to bend to the wills of those who are more criminally accomplished. While many offenders possess pro-social values, once incarcerated they may have little choice but to adopt the negative attitudes of those institutional peers that are more criminally and violently inclined. Within the prison, the term peer assumes a broad meaning. One's institutional peers are not limited to those with whom one directly associates but by default includes all those of a similar status. This shared status creates a homogenous community making it especially difficult for positively oriented inmates to withstand pressure to conform to the expectation espoused by the inmate culture.

It has also been observed that human behavior is influenced by the dominant values, norms and beliefs present within one's environment. Research reveals that peers have a significant influence on the development of behavioral patterns. If one's environment includes positive and nurturing peers that ascribe to socially productive values, one's behavior is likely to be positive and nurturing, but if one's environment is negatively charged, then one's behavior is likely to be negatively oriented. This dynamic may prove to be especially problematic for the young and inexperienced offender who finds him/herself in prison. Forcing offenders who may possess a pro-social orientation to integrate into a negatively oriented culture may ultimately be a socially destructive practice. The consequences of this practice may extend beyond the prison's walls, forever forging a negative link between the ex-inmate and his/her institutional peers. And similar to particle entanglement, this link may withstand the effects of both time and distance, influencing one's actions well into the future. If such a dynamic is at work, it can be manipulated and used for our collective benefit. For example, peer influence can also be positive in nature and can, therefore, be used to promote lawfulness among ex-inmates. The key to harnessing the power of peer influence is to create a positive and supportive correctional environment where the values of treatment and the benefits of rehabilitation are fully recognized.

Practitioners at the Elmira Reformatory were not shy in expressing their belief that they would have experienced greater success with offender reform had they separated amenable inmates from those who opposed treatment. They surmised that this separation might have eliminated opportunities for malleable inmates to be coerced, intimidated, corrupted or otherwise victimized. In fact, it is perfectly reasonable to believe that negatively oriented inmates are still exercising a great deal of influence over those who are less criminally experienced. Why might this be the case? Well, an incentive exists for positively oriented inmates to assume a negative orientation in an attempt to blend into a culture that demands conformity. The allure of assimilation is strong since it results in acceptance, access to goods and services, mitigates the pains of imprisonment and ultimately proves necessary for survival. The "pains of imprisonment" are often considered to be a loss of:

- freedom, movement and personal choice,
- unrestricted communications,
- personal safety and security,
- privacy, and
- access to heterosexual relationships.

While assimilation into this culture does not eliminate these pains, it does reduce discomfort while providing a degree of personal safety. The problem with assimilation is that it is predicated on the requirement that members oppose all forms of correctional authority. When considering the plight of the offender, we must acknowledge that:

- some are more criminally experienced than are others,
- some are more criminally inclined than are others,
- some have adopted an anti-social orientation prior to imprisonment while others have not, and
- some are receptive to treatment and warrant protection from negative influences.

Upon recognizing that there are positively and negatively oriented inmates, it then becomes prudent to create prisons designed to specifically meet the unique needs of each group. For positively oriented inmates, prisons would be characterized by ample opportunity for treatment, therapy and education.

These prisons would promote a positively charged peer culture where inmates would observe, encourage and support one another in their pursuit of personal reform. For negatively oriented inmates, prisons would be a safe and secure environment where needs could be met in an efficient manner. In these prisons, few overall resources would be devoted to rehabilitation since to do so would prove financially and operationally irresponsible. The separation of these two groups would effectively serve to insulate positively oriented inmates from those destructive influences that currently dominate the prison's culture.

Conclusion

Numerous perspectives in both the physical and social sciences attest to the potentially negative effects of environment and peer influence on human behavior. Most inmates eventually return to society with a majority of them being re-arrested shortly after release. Citizens would undoubtedly agree that high recidivism rates are unacceptable. Perhaps re-offending rates would decrease if officials were to create prisons where a positive and supportive culture promoted and reinforced therapeutic efforts. Such an approach is consistent with society's interest in having officials provide treatment as a means to reduce crime.

Furthermore, imprisonment will continue to be ineffective at breaking the crime cycle until the indiscriminate mixing of inmates cease. Perhaps this cycle can be broken if treatment is provided to positively oriented inmates in a friendly, supportive and nurturing environment. While a majority of Americans support treatment for prisoners, we must also recognize the existence of negatively oriented inmates who actively seek to corrupt the treatment process. For them, simple confinement appears most appropriate.

For centuries the great thinkers of physics have sought to advance our understanding of the natural world. This pursuit has taken a great deal of effort, innovation, creativity and interdisciplinary insight before success was achieved. No less daunting is the task of creating an effective prison system. Perhaps the atom and the prison are comparable since each is comprised of positively and negatively oriented elements whose proper management serves the greater social good. While the task at hand is formidable, the first step in breaking the crime cycle appears quite simple - insulate those inmates who are positively oriented from those who are not. In the next chapter, the laws of thermodynamics and motion are used to examine the prison and its operations. It is within this framework that the flow of energy is considered in greater detail. Furthermore, correctional mass is viewed as a significant determinant in the prison's reduction and elimination of treatment programs. Conclusions are then drawn with regard to the prison's declining energy levels and its current state of entropy.

HIGHLIGHTS

- Overlap exists between all academic fields with none being able to claim a monopoly on information or how it may be used to improve the human condition.
- Interdisciplinarity is a term that refers to combining two or more academic disciplines in such a way that increased insight is obtained into a particular area of interest.
- Physicists and penologists both engage in environmental manipulation.
- Inmate populations have grown exponentially over the past 30 years.
- The cost of operating America's correctional system now exceeds $60 billion a year.
- Quantum mechanics is a specialized branch of physics that studies the relationship between energy and matter at the atomic level.
- If *observation* can affect particle behavior then it is reasonable to assume that it can also affect human behavior and can, therefore, be manipulated to produce positive results.
- If *relationships* can affect particle behavior, then it is possible that they can also affect human behavior and can, therefore, be manipulated to produce positive results.
- Hawthorne has become synonymous with behavioral changes resulting from observation, environmental manipulation and increased expectations.
- An assessment of an offender's level of experience provides insight into the extent to which he/she has matured within the criminal lifestyle.
- As assessment of an offender's momentum provides insight into his/her attitude about criminality and correctional intervention.
- The nucleus serves as the unifying force around which particles congregate; the prison serves a similar function by making congregation and interaction possible among offenders (our particles).

- The proton, since it carries a positive charge is comparable to those inmates who have not fully committed themselves to a criminal lifestyle and are amenable toward treatment.

- Since the electron caries a negative charge it is comparable to those inmates who embrace criminality and disavow treatment.

- The probability that incarceration will produce law abiding behaviors among ex-inmates increases when observation within the prison is combined with environmental modification and increased expectation.

- Energy and peer influence have similar properties and are functional equivalents.

- When opposite charges or orientations are present within a system (be it in the atomic or penal realm), energy and peer influence tend to flow in one direction - from the negative toward the positive state.

- It has long been observed that prior to imprisonment, offenders and non-offenders tend to hold similar values with offenders engaging in conventional behaviors a majority of the time.

- Experienced and violent inmates have created a prison culture that rejects all authority that is not inmate based.

- An inmate's institutional peers are not limited to those with whom he/she directly associates but by default includes all those of a similar status.

- Numerous perspectives in both the physical and social sciences attest to the effects of environment and peer influence on behavior.

- Recidivism rates would decrease if officials were to create prisons where a positive and supportive culture promotes and reinforces therapeutic efforts.

- Socio-physics suggests that imprisonment will continue to be ineffective at breaking the crime cycle until the indiscriminate mixing of inmates cease.

- For centuries, noted scientists have sought to advance our understanding of the natural world. This pursuit has taken a great deal of effort before success was achieved. No less daunting is the task of creating an effective prison system.

- Forcing offenders who may possess a pro-social orientation to integrate into a negatively oriented culture may ultimately be a socially destructive practice.

- The first step in breaking the crime cycle appears quite simple, insulate those inmates who are positively oriented from those who are not.

QUESTIONS

1). Do you agree with the assertion that overlap exists between all academic fields with none being able to claim a monopoly on information or how it may be used to improve the human condition? Explain.

2). Has correctional thinking stagnated? Explain. What are the operational advantages/disadvantages to innovative and creative correctional thinking? Explain.

3). Why are treatment programs considered "non-essential" from an operational and budgetary perspective? Explain.

4). How is the Heisenberg Uncertainty Principle applicable to the prison? Explain.

5). How is the Hawthorne Effect applicable to the prison? Explain.

6). Is there a social equivalent to quantum entanglement? Explain.

7). Is there a value in visualizing offenders as being positively or negatively charged particles? Explain.

8). Generally speaking, do offenders and non-offenders have similar values? How might this possibility be used to promote rehabilitation? Explain. What ramifications exist (if any) for continuing to house amenable and nonamenable inmates within the same prisons? What ramifications exist (if any) for housing amenable and nonamenable inmates within separate prisons?

CHAPTER FIVE
Thermodynamics and Newtonian Motion: The Effects of Energy, Entropy and Mass on Rehabilitation

All serious attempts to advance our understanding of humanity must take physical laws into consideration.

In the previous chapter, we compared sub-atomic particles to prisoners and in doing so used physics to obtain added insight into offender behavior. As that chapter developed, we became increasingly familiar with the contributions of many prominent physicists. We also grew keenly aware that commonalities exist between all academic fields and came to regard the lines that have traditionally separated the sciences as arbitrary partitions that must be crossed if we are to increase our understanding of the social world.

Furthermore, it was within that chapter where we compared the prison to an atom's nucleus, surmising that each serves as a point of congregation and interaction. The proton, since it is positively charged, was likened to those inmates who have a favorable attitude toward treatment. Conversely, since the electron is negatively charged, it was compared to those inmates who oppose treatment. Likewise, negatively oriented inmates were viewed as having a detrimental influence on those with a positive orientation since energy and peer influence were considered equivalent and were hypothesized to flow from a negative toward a positive state. This flow was seen as impeding efforts at offender reform. To break this cycle an insulator was proposed to prevent negatively and positively oriented inmates from interacting. The similarities between the physical and social realms depicted in that chapter serve as the basis for the present effort.

Physicists have long suggested that connections exist between all fields, asserting that every serious attempt to advance our understanding of humanity must take physical laws into consideration. This assertion has become so widely accepted that there is a persistent belief that without physics, all scientific fields (including the social sciences) would suffer. In fact, in Peter Checkland's influential book, *Systems Thinking, Systems Practice* (1999), physics is frequently applied to the social sciences. Even renowned scholar Stephen Hawking acknowledges that a consideration of the natural sciences ideally allows us to better understand and predict human behavior.

In the pages that follow, the laws of thermodynamics (dealing with energy) and the laws of motion (pertaining to movement and force) are applied to the study of the prison. We selected these mainstays of physics after asking students to provide suggestions about those physical laws that they would like to see included in this chapter. We trusted that students would compile a list of laws that appear especially challenging for the task at hand. Once they made their suggestions, we agreed to select the two most frequent responses and surmised that to do so would provide a rigorous test of physics' ability to offer insight into prison operations.

In addition to determining if and to what extent thermodynamics and motion provide insight into the social realm, our intent as always is to encourage creative and innovative thinking. History demonstrates the importance of using imaginative and inventive means in our search for understanding. In fact, Albert Einstein, perhaps the most noted physicist of all time, openly endorsed interdisciplinary study and is credited with stating, "imagination is more important than knowledge". This statement emphasizes the importance for scholars to think in a broad, creative and intuitive fashion. Perhaps this chapter can make a positive contribution to this process by encouraging its readers to do the same. Creative and intuitive correctional thinking is of vital importance since the role played by the prison within our democracy is paramount to the recognition, promotion and protection of citizenship. Few institutions more directly reflect a nation's values or have a greater impact on public safety than does the prison. Therefore, any approach that increases our understanding of the prison's operations should be welcomed.

Before proceeding, keep in mind that those definitions previously provided with regard to penology, socio-physics and socio-physicists still apply. However, in addition to peer influence, the factors of interest, effort, time and resources will also be considered manifestations and functional equivalents of energy. Energy is the ability of an organism or physical system to achieve a specific objective. Each of these factors can be considered an equivalent to energy since each is necessary for the achievement of the prison's objectives. For example, to pursue offender rehabilitation, prison officials must first have an interest in doing so and then invest the required amounts of effort, time and resources toward its achievement. While the comparisons herein rely on observations, definitions and laws commonly associated with physics, they are nonetheless progressively applied to the social realm. And, while we have previously used physics to obtain greater insight into inmate behavior, our objective in this chapter is to explore the prison as a social system that, similar to its natural counterparts, is subject to physical laws.

Energy, Mass and Motion

Thermodynamics is the study of energy in the forms of heat, pressure and movement. The study of thermodynamics can be traced to the seventeenth century and to the efforts of Otto von Guericke, Robert Boyle and Robert Hook (among others). These early physicists observed that energy flows from a state of excitement toward a state of rest. For example, the steam that rises from a cup of hot tea (representing a state of excitement or higher energy) into the surrounding air (representing a state of rest or lower energy) is easily visible. In this example, the tea loses energy to its environment, which is visible in the form of rising steam. In time, the tea's temperature will equal that of the surrounding air. Conversely, if the cup contains iced tea, the process will be reversed and the flow of energy will be from the environment into the beverage as is demonstrated by the eventual melting of its ice. In this example, the tea represents a state of lower energy whereas the air represents a state of higher energy. Given time, the temperature of the tea will equal that of its environment. Both examples depict a transfer of energy between objects and environments with energy continually flowing from a higher to a lower level.

Physicists interested in thermodynamics pay particular attention to energy and how its movement influences system performance. A system is a set of components that collectively form an integrated whole. Each component has a functional as well as a structural relationship to the others, with all components being necessary for the achievement of a common objective. A system is considered open when exchanges of energy occur between itself and its environment and closed when little or no exchange occurs. Furthermore, a state of entropy is said to afflict a system when it functions improperly or performs at less than an optimal level. A consideration of energy and its movement within and between objects and systems is increasingly being used to explain the dynamics of social interaction.

In physics, Isaac Newton is considered a scientific luminary and will forever be associated with the laws of motion. Newton realized that the direction and momentum of an object (and for our purposes a system) remains unchanged unless otherwise acted upon. Likewise, an object (or a system) at rest tends to stay at rest, resisting movement. And, similar to the laws of thermodynamics which acknowledge the influence that energy has on the behaviors of objects and systems, Newton recognized that increases or decreases to an object's mass (or to a system's mass) will likely produce a corresponding change in behavior. He memorialized his ideas within *Mathematical Principles of Natural Philosophy* in 1687 (commonly referred to as the *Principia*). Collectively, the laws of thermodynamics and motion suggest that:

- energy flows from a state of excitement toward a state of rest,
- the amount of energy available for use by an object or system often varies and tends to dissipate over time,
- a system's level of entropy tends to increase over time,
- changes in mass and/or energy tend to produce changes in the behaviors of objects and systems, and
- an object or system, at rest or in motion, will remain so unless otherwise acted upon.

To determine the extent to which these observations apply to the present undertaking, we must consider the historical and contemporary nature of the prison. Detectable changes within the prison will provide insight into its use of energy, its level of entropy and how each may affect its operational and ideological orientations.

Rehabilitative Momentum

Penologists identify the prison's traditional objectives as rehabilitation, retribution, deterrence and incapacitation. Rehabilitation refers to the adoption of a pro-social orientation leading to a cessation of criminality. Retribution (closely related to revenge) seeks to harm an offender in a manner that is proportional to his/her crime (i.e. an eye for an eye). Retributive ideology asserts that certain behaviors render a perpetrator deserving of pain. Deterrence refers to a modification of one's behavior in order to avoid pain, whereas incapacitation seeks to eliminate one's ability to victimize society through separation and solitude (i.e. removal from society via jail or prison). While these objectives have collectively exerted a significant influence over the prison's activities, an assessment of rehabilitation more so than an evaluation of any other objective promises to provide relevant information about the prison's use of energy and how energy has affected its operational and ideological underpinnings. Why? Since rehabilitation is a proactive pursuit requiring an effort by officials and inmates alike, its achievement is much more energy and resource dependent than are the prison's other objectives. Therefore, a consideration of energy proves crucial to an increased understanding of the prison and its behaviors.

When considering rehabilitation, it is evident that its pursuit was traditionally viewed as a crime preventative and a promoter of public health. An interest in rehabilitation is painstakingly detailed in William Paley's *Principles of Moral and Political Philosophy* (1785). Paley, a noted English philosopher and religious leader (1743-1805), wrote extensively on the subjects of free will and repentance. Paley's efforts helped promote rehabilitation and ensured that offender reform held a place of prominence in the early prison system of colonial America. For example, in 1787 a group of colonial leaders, many of whom we recognize today, met at the home of Benjamin Franklin and endorsed rehabilitation as the primary pursuit of the prison. Then in 1870, at a meeting of the National Prison Association (an organization now known as the American Correctional Association), penologists reaffirmed the importance of rehabilitation. These endorsements assured the prominence of rehabilitation in American penology for nearly two centuries.

The pursuit of rehabilitation was not openly challenged until the latter half of the twentieth century when two large and exceptionally violent riots cast doubt on the prison's ability to promote inmate reform. The first of these riots occurred in 1971 at the Attica Correctional Facility located in upstate New York. During this riot, 43 individuals were killed. Media accounts of this event portrayed inmates as brutal, inhumane and unworthy of educational, vocational and therapeutic provisions. This riot, more so than any previous uprising, forced the public to acknowledge the increasingly squalid conditions and the brutal environment of the prison. The second riot occurred at the Penitentiary of New Mexico located in Santa Fe (1980) and resulted in the deaths of 33 inmates. Often considered the most violent and destructive riot in American history, Santa Fe came to symbolize the hopelessness of correctional intervention. Its timing solidified the decade old movement against rehabilitation that had, by this time, gained considerable political momentum. These riots helped create a perception that America's prisons were on the brink of anarchy and collapse. In fact, nearly 60% of all twentieth century riots occurred after 1970 with approximately 40% of them occurring in the 1980s alone. Collectively, these riots were used by get-tough proponents to solicit support for their position. Robert Martinson, an outspoken opponent of therapeutic initiatives, became famous for authoring the *Nothing Works* report (1974). Its title became the mantra for those who sought to abolish treatment initiatives. Martinson's position was supported by other noted criminologists including James Q. Wilson (1975) and David Fogel (1975), each of whom similarly demanded that the prison free itself from a treatment ideology. It was their considered opinion that the prison should focus exclusively on its ability to incapacitate offenders and to do so in the cheapest manner possible.

Correctional Mass

In this section the phrase correctional mass is used to refer to the size of the prisoner population. As we have seen, mass is a vital consideration since it may affect a system's ability to accomplish its objective in an efficient and effective manner. This is particularly true of the prison where mass impacts all areas of institutional operations and continues to shape the relationship that exists between the prison and the inmate population. Of particular importance is the relationship between mass and rehabilitation.

Contemporary scholars often ignore the historical relationship between rehabilitation and imprisonment. Instead, they tend to portray the prison as an institution whose sole purpose is, and will always be, punishment. This portrayal, which conveniently disavows treatment, has been actively buttressed by the courts. For example, in *Mistretta v. United States* (1989) the U.S. Supreme Court declared that the federal judiciary would no longer consider rehabilitation during sentencing processes. This declaration was made during a time when the number of offenders being sent to prison was reaching epidemic proportions, a clear indication that the judiciary had embraced incarceration as the sanction du jour. Nearly 1 out of every 100 adults is now behind bars, a rate that is 5 to 8 times higher than that of other developed nations. Currently, state and federal prisons house about 1.7 million individuals compared to about 250,000 in 1980. The probability for an American citizen to be incarcerated during his/her lifetime tripled between 1974 and 2001.

Consider further that between 1985 and 2004 state correctional expenditures increased dramatically, yet treatment initiatives were simultaneously reduced and, at times, even eliminated out of financial necessity. In other words, while expenditures increased, spending on treatment decreased. In fact, one state even considered terminating all of its full time prison educators as a way to further reduce its operating budget. Judicial and legislative actions have done little to help address this issue. Returning to our consideration of the judiciary, we see that in 1980 alone, approximately half of those offenders convicted in federal court were sentenced to prison. By 2001, that number had risen to nearly 80%, an increase of about thirty-percent. Comparable trends have been observed at the state level where nearly seven out of every ten convicted felons now receive a term of incarceration. Moreover, the length of time that is served prior to release has also increased. At the federal level, the typical inmate now serves 90% of his/her sentence prior to release. Similarly, from 1990 to 2009, the average state inmate's length of stay increased by about thirty-percent. There are extremes, however. For example, the typical Florida inmate has seen his/her length of confinement increase by 166% over the past twenty years. Truth in sentencing laws now require most state inmates to serve a greater proportion of their sentence before becoming parole-eligible.

In spite of judicial and legislative actions, nearly 90% of all Americans still support treatment for prisoners. Nonetheless, it is difficult to locate information on those treatment programs that still exist and even more difficult to locate information on their effectiveness as measured by recidivism rates. This is due to a growing uncertainty about how to measure recidivism. For example, researchers often measure recidivism by re-arrest, re-conviction or re-incarceration - making it especially difficult to compare results. Of the three methods commonly used to measure recidivism, re-arrest is the most comprehensive since it remains free of judicial and correctional manipulation. When considering re-arrest rates, in 1983, approximately 63% of all ex-inmates were arrested within three years of release, increasing to 68% by 1994. Increases in the arrests of former inmates have subsequently led to increases in conviction and confinement rates. For example, the proportion of former inmates returning to federal prison within 3 years of release increased by nearly 7% between 1986 and 1994. Currently, about 70% of all ex-inmates return to state custody within 3 years of release, up from about 33% in the early 1980s. In spite of these discouraging statistics, studies of existing programs consistently show that treatment can reduce recidivism rates by ten percent to twenty percent. In fact, one treatment program in California produced a return to custody rate of less than 11% (a decrease of 59%). Similarly, a recent multi-state study found that inmate participation in treatment produced a 9% reduction in re-arrest rates, an 8% reduction in re-conviction rates, and a decrease of 10% in re-incarceration rates during the three years following release. These studies suggest that a treatment ideology, which manifests itself in therapeutic initiatives, can have a direct effect on recidivism rates, helping create a safer society. However, a recurrent theme voiced by correctional administrators nationwide is that the prison's current mass makes it nearly impossible for them to treat inmate populations.

A Return to Physical Laws

Having briefly reviewed the laws of thermodynamics and motion, it now becomes necessary to explain how these laws pertain to penology. These laws suggest that:

- an aging prison system will gravitate toward a low energy state. In this respect, the prison is similar to other objects/systems. Rehabilitation is a proactive pursuit that requires large amounts of sustainable energy. In fact, of all the prison's objectives, rehabilitation is the most energy dependent. The low energy state of the modern prison is reflected in its reduction and in some cases its elimination of treatment initiatives,
- an aging prison system will gravitate toward an entropic state. Entropy as used herein, suggests a loss of effectiveness. When viewed in this manner, the prison is similar to all other objects/systems and is becoming incrementally less effective at achieving its primary objective of breaking the crime cycle. Increases in recidivism rates among former inmates provide a gauge by which the prison's effectiveness can be determined,
- when an object/system gains or loses mass, its behavior is affected. A prison's mass is equivalent to the size of its inmate population. Recent population increases have directly contributed to reductions in therapeutic initiatives, revealing a direct cause and effect relationship. Conversely, a future decrease in mass may permit the prison's behaviors to more closely approximate those of its pre-expansion state, and
- an object/system at rest or in motion will remain so unless forced to act otherwise. To behave in any other manner requires a significant expenditure of energy either to accelerate or decelerate the object/system or to alter its trajectory. If future treatment initiatives are to gain momentum, a substantial investment of energy will be required.

We must now confess that we were deceptive in our previous assertion that all systems are susceptible to energy loss and entropy. Generally speaking, only closed systems are at risk for these fates since their ability to draw energy from their environments is negligible. Yet, it doesn't appear that the prison is completely a closed system nor does it appear to be exclusively an open system.

Instead, the prison displays traits common to each. Consider for example that the prison as a closed system operates in an isolated fashion, having limited interaction with its environment. In fact, prison officials have long operated under the hands-off doctrine. This doctrine, popularized by the U.S. Supreme Court's ruling in *Pervear v. Massachusetts* (1886) and reaffirmed in the Prison Litigation Reform Act (1995), shields the actions of prison administrators from external review and intervention, greatly reducing the number of exchanges that occur between the prison and society. However, the prison can also be considered an open system since it will, given the proper conditions, interact with the public. These interactions are limited, highly controlled and include furloughs, work release and public outreach programs. Furthermore, a majority of all inmates are eventually paroled or discharged, representing the largest and most enduring exchange that occurs between the prison and society. In other words, there is a constant flow of offenders into and out of the prison. The prison, therefore, exhibits a duality in its nature - it operates under the specter of isolation and limited social interaction, but engages in various activities where exchanges are inevitable.

While the prison may be suffering from decreasing energy levels and increased entropy, an almost inexplicable immunity appears to have protected its ideological orientation from a similar fate. Prison officials have not yet completely jettisoned rehabilitation as an operational ideology with this hesitancy perhaps being linked to the public's ongoing interest in and support of treatment. This immunity suggests that there may be multiple energies at work including those that influence the prison's operations (political) and those that influence its philosophy (popular). Nonetheless, there appears to be a disjunction between the prison's practices and its current ideological orientation.

Conclusion

Massive inmate populations continue to result in a redistribution of resources and a reordering of the prison's operational priorities. This has forced prison officials to embrace a more simplistic administrative approach that relies more heavily on passive rather than active pursuits. In essence, the prison has moved toward the lower end of the energy spectrum where efforts designed to break the crime cycle have been curtailed; yet, public support for rehabilitation endures. Whether therapeutic initiatives will be re-energized and pursued in the future remains unknown. However, such an event, were it to gain sufficient momentum, would likely require a simultaneous decrease in correctional mass and a substantial and sustained investment of energy. Provided a decrease in prison mass could be achieved, current levels of public support appear capable of supplying the energy necessary to power treatment initiatives. What remains unknown is whether political figures would allocate the funding necessary to fuel these initiatives.

While many contemporary researchers still ignore the natural sciences as a mechanism to gain insight into human and institutional behavior, other scholars are broadening their approaches in an attempt to obtain a more comprehensive understanding of the social realm. Socio-physics encourages the development of creative, innovative and interdisciplinary modes of inquiry and in doing so, promises to help advance our understanding of how energy, entropy and mass affect the prison.

In the next chapter you will be introduced to chaos theory. Chaos within the prison can be visualized as a disjunction that exists between the public's expectations and the actual effects of incarceration. Chaoticians recognize that all systems are sensitive to environmental conditions. Even subtle changes to an environment can lead to significant inconsistencies in the actions and outcomes of a system. This has substantial ramifications for social systems since they are intended to produce uniform and positive results among a heterogeneous clientele.

While the level of chaos existing within the contemporary prison is considered significant, it is suggested that it can be reduced through intelligent and deliberate action.

HIGHLIGHTS

- The lines that have traditionally separated the sciences are arbitrary partitions that must be crossed if we are to increase our understanding of the social world.

- Physicists have long suggested that connections exist between all fields, asserting that every serious attempt to advance our understanding of humanity must take physical laws into consideration.

- History demonstrates the importance of using imaginative and inventive means in our search for understanding.

- The role of the prison within our democracy is paramount to the recognition, promotion and protection of citizenship.

- Interest, effort, time and resources are manifestations and functional equivalents of energy since they are necessary for the achievement of the prison's objectives.

- Thermodynamics is the study of energy in the forms of heat, pressure and movement.

- Energy always flows from a state of excitement toward a state of rest.

- A system is a set of components that collectively form an integrated whole. Each component has a functional as well as a structural relationship to the others, with all components being necessary for the achievement of a common objective.

- Physicists interested in thermodynamics pay particular attention to energy and how its movement and transfer affect system performance.

- A system is considered open when exchanges of energy occur between itself and its environment.

- A system is considered closed when few exchanges of energy occur between itself and its environment.

- Entropy afflicts a system when it functions improperly or performs at less than an optimal level.

- A consideration of energy and its movement within and between objects and systems is increasingly being used to explain the dynamics of social interaction.

- The direction and momentum of an object (or a system) remains unchanged unless otherwise acted upon.

- Increases or decreases to an object's mass (or to a system's mass) will likely produce a corresponding change in behavior.

- An assessment of rehabilitation, more so than an evaluation of any other objective, promises to provide relevant information about the prison's operational and ideological underpinnings.

- Since rehabilitation is a proactive pursuit requiring a concentrated effort by officials and inmates alike, its achievement is more energy and resource dependent than are other objectives.

- When considering rehabilitation it is evident that its pursuit was traditionally viewed as a crime-preventative and a promoter of public health.

- In 1787, a group of colonial leaders met at the home of Benjamin Franklin and endorsed rehabilitation as the primary purpose of the prison.

- Nearly 60% of all twentieth century riots occurred after 1970, with approximately 40% of them occurring in the 1980s alone.

- Robert Martinson, an outspoken opponent of therapeutic initiatives, became famous for authoring the *Nothing Works* report.

- Contemporary scholars often ignore the historical relationship between rehabilitation and imprisonment, choosing instead to portray the prison as an institution whose sole purpose is, and will always be, punishment.

- The probability for an American citizen to be imprisoned during his/her lifetime tripled between 1974 and 2001.

- Currently, America's correctional system costs taxpayers about $60 billion annually.

- Nearly 90% of all Americans support treatment for prisoners.

- Of the three methods commonly used to measure recidivism, re-arrest is the most comprehensive since it remains free of judicial and correctional manipulation.
- About 70% of all ex-inmates return to state custody within 3 years of their release, up from about 33% in the early 1980s.
- Studies of existing programs consistently show that treatment can reduce recidivism rates by 10% to 20%.
- The prison is similar to other objects/systems and tends to lose energy over time.
- An aging prison system will gravitate toward an entropic state.
- Recent increases in the inmate population have contributed to reductions in therapeutic initiatives, revealing a cause and effect relationship.
- Prison officials have long operated under the protection of the hands-off doctrine. This doctrine shields the actions of prison administrators from external review and intervention.
- The prison exhibits a duality in its nature - it operates under the specter of isolation and limited social interaction but engages in various activities where exchanges with its environment are inevitable.

QUESTIONS

1). Do you agree or disagree with the statement "that imagination is more important than knowledge" when attempting to improve our understanding of human and institutional behavior? Explain.

2). Are the factors of interest, effort, time and resources functional equivalents of energy? Explain.

3). The observation was made that energy flows from a state of excitement toward a state of rest. Does the same hold true for the various forms of social energy (as listed above in question #2)? Explain.

4). Compare and contrast open and closed systems. Which of these more closely describes the contemporary prison? Why?

5). Does a system's level of entropy increase over time? Explain. How does entropy affect the prison? Explain.

6). How accurate is the suggestion that rehabilitation is a proactive pursuit whose achievement is more energy and resource dependent than are other correctional objectives? Explain.

7). Explain the impact of the Attica and New Mexico prison riots on the public's perception of inmates. Did these events have positive or negative consequences for treatment initiatives?

8). Currently 70% of all ex-inmates return to state custody within three years of release, up from about 33% in the early 1980s. What is responsible for this increase? List those factors that lend credibility to your response.

CHAPTER SIX
Chaos Theory

Disorder gives rise to order - and from order springs chaos.
One precedes the other and neither exists alone.

Having recently been introduced to chaos theories, we have naturally asked ourselves if these theories can increase our understanding of human and institutional behavior. In essence, what insight if any can chaos theory provide about penology? To make this chapter more reader-friendly, we will treat all chaos theories as a single approach. This is possible since chaos theories, whether they are biologically, mathematically or philosophically oriented, share a set of basic principles that we will introduce shortly. Furthermore, since we seek to provide little more than an introduction to chaos theory we do not need to be as precise in our descriptions as do those scholars who conduct research based upon this theoretical framework. Our approach relies heavily upon chaos theory as it was originally developed and applied to environmental systems. Therefore, the prison will be viewed as a system operating within a complex environment.

To make a determination about whether chaos theory can be applied to penology it first becomes necessary to understand the meaning of "chaos". This, as its name suggests is not an easy task. In fact, chaos theories are among the most complicated we have yet encountered. It seems that "chaos" certainly lives up to its namesake! To state the obvious, the term chaos suggests that events are occurring in a disordered, haphazard and unpredictable fashion. It is for these reasons that chaos is always perceived as undesirable. In essence, when a chaotic state develops, a system's actions become less effective. Part and parcel to this perspective is the observation that systems are highly sensitive to the conditions in which they operate. Small differences in these conditions (be they internally or externally situated) can create unanticipated outcomes. When considering social systems, these conditions may be related to individual-level factors that include experience, emotion, cognitive development and amenability. At the institutional level these factors include ideological orientation, access to appropriate personnel and economic realities. Furthermore, there are factors including politics that affect both individual and institutional level conditions.

At the heart of chaos theory is an acknowledgement that as a system operates (whether in the natural or social realm), its actions and its associated outcomes often become more disordered and less predictable over time. Imagine a young system. As this system operates, its actions and its related outcomes are relatively uniform and predictable. However, as operations continue and as greater amounts of time pass, the likelihood for environmental conditions to affect operations increases. In the prison (a mature system), chaos can be visualized as a disjunction existing between the expectations of the taxpaying public and the actual effects that stem from incarceration. Stated a bit differently, any social system plagued by chaos will inevitably produce outcomes that are not aligned with the public's expectations or its welfare. In other words, chaotic prison systems fail to rehabilitate inmates while ignoring established organizational, operational and theoretical frameworks. Since chaos always hinders a system's effectiveness, ongoing performance evaluations become increasingly necessary. The prison's performance has traditionally been determined by considering recidivism rates. They are the only measure by which both actions and outcomes can be comprehensively assessed. It is also through a measure of recidivism that the degree of chaos present within our correctional institutions is revealed. In short, a properly operating prison system will produce low recidivism rates whereas a chaotic prison system will be plagued by exceptionally high recidivism rates. It is worth repeating that a system's actions and its corresponding outcomes are directly linked to internal and external conditions as well as the length of time that the system has been in operation (more on the "time" factor shortly).

The Butterfly Effect

A system's sensitivity to environmental conditions and the ability of these conditions to influence actions and outcomes is often referred to as the "butterfly effect". In fact, this phrase formed part of the title to a paper authored by MIT professor Edward Lorenz in 1972. In his paper, Lorenz raised the question about whether a butterfly flapping its wings on one side of the earth might cause a large-scale event (perhaps a storm with hurricane force winds) to occur in some far off location, perhaps on the other side of the globe. Of course, the insect's flapping wings represent a minor alteration to the environmental conditions of a system that eventually result in changing the very nature of the system itself. Had the butterfly never flapped its wings, perhaps the event on the opposite side of the earth would have never occurred - or had it, perhaps it might have occurred differently.

One could also speculate about how the characteristics of the butterfly might have affected our event. What if the size of the insect varied? What effect if any would an increase or decrease in the number of wing-flaps occurring per minute have had? What if there had been a change in the direction that our insect was traveling? Would these factors, had they varied, resulted in a different outcome? For example, if the butterfly was of a large variety, perhaps a Queen Alexandra's Birdwing (with a wing span of 12 inches), would the event have been more intense than if our butterfly was of a smaller variety like the Western Pygmy Blue (with a wingspan of just half an inch)? What if the butterfly in question was of a yellow variety instead of a green variety? Would the event have occurred differently? And what if our insect took flight on a sunny day versus a cloudy day, or on a warm day versus a cool day? Would these conditions have affected our storm?

The point we are making is that there are many factors that can and do affect the actions and outcomes of systems. Add "time" to this mix and events become even less predictable. Why? Well, time provides an opportunity for localized environmental conditions to disperse throughout a system, exponentially enhancing their collective ability to affect outcome. When this occurs (as in our butterfly example), it often results in a system's actions becoming inconsistent, thereby hindering our ability to accurately predict results. Vital to all chaos perspectives is recognition that changes in the conditions of a system (whether they are internally or externally situated) can have a huge impact on outcome. Such a consideration proves critical when dealing with social systems that are intended to produce uniform and positive results among a heterogeneous clientele.

Social and Natural Systems Compared

Modern institutions are increasingly being viewed as complex social systems that share characteristics with those systems found within the natural realm. All systems whether they are of the natural or social variety are subject to environmental conditions or forces that are precursors to chaos. For our purpose, we will limit our consideration to social systems. When doing so, please note that:

- all social systems are vulnerable to the influence of internal and external conditions/forces,
- this vulnerability makes social systems susceptible to chaos,
- since all social systems have been created by humans, are operated by humans and serve humanity, they must be considered extremely complex,
- complexity (arising out of perceptions, beliefs, opinions and interactions) produces a great deal of bias, misinformation,

distortions of fact and error (all of which have a detrimental effect on a system's actions and outcomes),

- even subtle changes to a system's environmental conditions, although perceived perhaps as being inconsequential, can lead to significant inconsistencies in the actions and outcomes of that system (in essence, repeated iteration will produce divergent and unpredictable outcomes),
- divergent and unpredictable outcomes may lead to a decreased investment in a system (i.e. a reduction in the interest, effort, time and resources being devoted to it), and
- this, in turn, becomes both a symptom as well as a producer of chaos.

Chaos, as we define it, is an inability or even an outright refusal by prison officials to utilize resources to break the crime cycle. As such, chaos is reflected in the distance that the prison has placed between itself and offender rehabilitation. If you doubt that the prison is in a chaotic state, consider the increasing number of statements being made by correctional officials in which they blatantly ignore or otherwise downplay the ineffectiveness of modern correctional practices. Prison officials are increasingly unable to communicate the benefits of imprisonment in light of absurdly high recidivism rates. These rates and the inability of officials to explain the social benefits of incarceration (beyond incapacitation) clearly suggest that the prison is in a chaotic state. In essence, the taxpayer expects imprisonment to break the crime cycle yet the contemporary prison is doing little to accomplish this objective.

If you recall from previously in this book, one of the earliest indications that chaos was beginning to spread throughout the prison system is found in the writings of Robert Martinson. His writings were a reflection of and a mechanism for the spread of chaos. As an outspoken opponent of therapeutic initiatives, he became famous for his *Nothing Works* report. The phrase "nothing works" became the mantra for those who considered the prison incapable of rehabilitating offenders. Martinson's position was supported by other academicians including

James Q. Wilson and David Fogel. Each of these acclaimed criminologists demanded that the prison free itself from any and all expectations pertaining to offender rehabilitation. It was their considered opinion that the prison should focus exclusively on its ability to incapacitate offenders. Supporters of this approach suggested that such a move was necessary because offenders were losing interest in treatment. They claimed that this disinterest rendered treatment unnecessary. Of course, the confusion caused by urging the prison to break from its traditional objectives was both a symptom and a producer of chaos.

Proponents of Martinson's approach effectively sought to eliminate all non-essential services with education, training and therapy being considered "non-essential". If inmates were going to act in an unpredictable and violent fashion (as proponents of this approach claimed was occurring in increasing numbers), then they should be dealt with accordingly. The prison would no longer pursue an outcome intended for the long-term benefit of society but would instead focus exclusively upon the here-and-now (a reactive and short-sighted strategy). It is interesting to note that an increase in the frequency of prison riots occurring during this era was not itself considered a result of this movement but was instead viewed as its justification. Advocates of this movement were essentially creating a prison system whereby the effects of incarceration upon inmate behavior would be determined by fate and not by effort or investment. A natural by-product of this orientation was a growing indifference by officials with regard to the prison's culture. Officials would no longer seek to control this culture but would instead by their acquiescence effectively relinquish much of their control to inmate leadership. Both liberals and conservatives alike embraced this approach without regard for its consequences. Of course, since treatment lacked support from either political party, anti-treatment perspectives were further legitimized. Thus, prison officials began to adopt a cold, detached and sterile approach.

This change, though it started small, gained considerable momentum over time and much like our butterfly, has created a major disturbance that has impacted the correctional environment. Consider, for example, that this disturbance has produced unforeseen outcomes including:

- a rapid and unprecedented increase in the inmate population,
- a rapid and unprecedented rise in prison construction,
- a partnership with the private sector to build and operate prisons for the government,
- a rapid and unprecedented influx of new staff into our nation's prisons that did not have a genuine interest in corrections - nor did many of them have the qualifications to become effective leaders within the field. In other words, a large percentage of this new staff were not invested in corrections as a long-term career but rather accepted employment as a stop-gap measure, biding time until something else materialized - essentially creating a transient workforce,
- an inmate population that became more defiant/resistant toward correctional authority, openly questioning the prison's legitimacy (inmates came to view the prison's actions as self-serving and undertaken with little or no concern for their welfare), and
- an intensification of interest among prison authorities in security and budgetary issues while simultaneously ignoring ways to protect, educate and rehabilitate amenable prisoners.

While these outcomes may have been unforeseen due to an eagerness to embrace the "nothing works" orientation, a change in the correctional environment has nonetheless forced the prison into a chaotic state that is further reflected in:

- the absence of a core set of operational philosophies that clearly promote public safety,
- a continuing refusal by correctional authorities to acknowledge traditional ideological underpinnings,
- the systematic and ongoing removal by prison officials of departmental terminology pertaining to rehabilitation, treatment, education and therapy,

- an operational perspective that asserts that the prison's social value is directly dependent on its ability to hold massive inmate populations,
- a growing desire by authorities to use internal characteristics to assess the prison's performance (since they are more easily manipulated and controlled) rather than to use recidivism (an external characteristic) to determine the prison's social value,
- a refusal by officials to consider the prison's actions (or inactions) as a public health and safety issue,
- an orientation that foregoes proactive efforts to break the crime cycle, replacing them instead with a laissez-faire reliance on fate, and
- elevated recidivism rates.

These observations provide a good indication about the extent to which chaos permeates the prison system. When considering these factors, it becomes clear that every area related to prison operations is now affected by disorder. And while this hampers the prison's ability to effectively break the crime cycle, it has also contributed to the huge financial costs associated with supporting a system where the average offender commonly serves multiple terms of incarceration during his/her lifetime. By visualizing our prisons as having revolving doors, citizens become sensitized to the fact that more often than not, newly released inmates will reoffend and become institutionalized again and again and again. However, the real problem with permitting the prison to operate in such a manner is that at some point chaos may become the new normal. This would have a devastating impact on the frequency and duration of pro-treatment periods (i.e. our correctional pendulum). Of course, at some point, chaos may increase to such a level that a complete and permanent loss of all treatment rationale occurs.

Actions, Outcomes and Predictions

The effects of chaos are similar regardless of the system under consideration. For example, chaos creates divergent and unpredictable results whether it exists within a social or natural system. The difficulty in forecasting weather patterns is an appropriate example of how chaos affects a natural system. In fact, chaos theory was created to help explain the inaccuracies inherent in making predictions about changes in atmospheric conditions. While we can, with a great deal of accuracy, predict short-term weather patterns, we are less accurate when making long-term forecasts. This is due to the effect that environmental variables have on the development of weather patterns. Any single environmental variable (including pressure, temperature and humidity) can produce changes in the weather, and when these variables exert their collective influence, predictions become problematic. Time compounds this effect by giving variables the opportunity to combine and recombine in unique ways with each permutation having a differing effect on the weather. The more time existing between a prediction and the event being predicted, the more inaccurate weather forecasts become. In other words, it is nearly impossible to predict weather patterns accurately beyond a few days into the future.

Chaos within a social system behaves in a similar way and is evidenced in those outcomes that often run contrary to the health and wellbeing of society. Just as we understand how atmospheric conditions affect weather, we must also develop a greater understanding of how institutional conditions affect the future behaviors of ex-inmates. And similar to atmospheric conditions where cause-and-effect relationships are understood but where specific long-term predictions become problematic, we must similarly develop an understanding of the cause-and-effect relationship that may exist between a prison's environment and the future actions of its former inmates. While progressive penologists understand that the prison's actions influence the behaviors of ex-inmates, long-term predictions about these effects remain contentious. What we cannot predict with any degree of certainty is:

- the frequency at which an ex-inmate will commit future crimes (although most will commit additional crimes and may do so with increasing frequency),
- the types of future crimes that an ex-inmate may engage in (although we know that imprisonment encourages criminal diversification),
- the specific impact that a crime will have upon a future victim(s), and
- the extent to which an ex-inmate may encourage criminality among those family members, peers and associates susceptible to such influence.

It becomes especially important for officials to understand that the prison's actions almost certainly have an affect on the future behaviors of ex-inmates (to assume anything less is irresponsible and jeopardizes public safety). By refusing to acknowledge this possibility, officials are excused from all deliberate and proactive attempts intended to break the crime cycle. The frequent changes that occur within the prison obscure this issue even further. Consider if you will the hypothetical pendulum that appears throughout this book? This pendulum sits on an uneven base. This causes its bob to favor one ideology more strongly than it does the other. During those times when our pendulum's bob favors a punitive sentiment, innovative and creative thoughts and practices become passé. It is at these times when the prison reduces or altogether ceases treatment efforts. Conversely, when a reform ideology is favored, innovative and creative thoughts and practices become prevalent. It is during these times that the prison openly embraces therapeutic pursuits. We are currently unable to predict when our pendulum's bob will change direction, the speed at which this change will occur or the duration of this change. This see-saw motion, however, keeps the prison in a state of limbo characterized by confusion and disorder. We remain confident based upon past events that the prison will again, in the near future, embrace a treatment perspective - but to what degree or under what circumstances this may happen remains unclear. However, with each subsequent change, the possibility exists that punitive periods may grow increasingly longer in duration while pro-treatment periods may become increasingly shorter. It would be beneficial for our pendulum to sit on an even base and for its bob to be at rest, indicating a balance in ideology.

While treatment has been proven to reduce recidivism rates, officials often make predictions about crime and disorder that are intentionally designed to create fear (this has proven to be an effective tool for securing increased state funding). When doing so, these officials fail to acknowledge that their predictions may be inaccurate or that rehabilitation largely reduces the need to anticipate future events or trends. For example, the rehabilitation of an inmate effectively eliminates the "unknown-factor" that is reflected in those bulleted items just presented. It is vital that we understand that variations in the frequency, nature and impact of future criminality are only considerations when dealing with active criminals and those who may be described as nonamenable. Rehabilitation is the only penal objective that reduces the "unknown" while ensuring that the prison's actions and its outcomes promote social health and wellbeing. In essence, rehabilitation reduces the effects of chaos at the individual level, and when accomplished on a large scale, results in a lowering of crime rates and correctional expenditures.

Having made these observations, it is important for the reader to have a clear understanding of how chaos theory relates to penology. Chaos theory:

- reveals the vulnerability of social systems to environmental conditions,
- reveals that even small, almost unperceivable changes can have dramatic effects upon a system's operations, and
- suggests that it is possible to eliminate disorder and reverse its effects through the manipulation of a system's environment. In other words, chaos within an artificial, man-made system exists solely because we allow it to exist.

If these observations are correct, then we have every reason to believe that it is possible to reduce the amount of chaos within the prison. How should we approach this task? Well, taking a lesson from Dr. Lorenz' own playbook, we need only to introduce a slight alteration into the correctional environment and wait for our changes to gain momentum. And just like our butterfly, given time, these intentional and deliberate alterations may have their desired effect. This suggests that the prison can again find balance and become an effective mechanism for breaking the crime cycle.

Conclusion

The term "chaos" is synonymous with events that occur in a disordered, haphazard and unpredictable fashion. Chaos is always perceived as undesirable since it produces inconsistent actions and erratic outcomes. Chaos Theory recognizes that even small variations occurring in a system's internal or external environments can produce widely divergent results. This sensitivity is often referred to as the "butterfly effect". Time compounds this effect by giving variables the opportunity to combine and recombine in unique ways with each permutation producing a differing result. This becomes an important consideration when dealing with social systems that are intended to produce uniform and positive results among a heterogeneous clientele. While Chaos Theory reveals the vulnerability of social systems to environmental conditions, it also suggests that small manipulations of a system's environment can yield substantial benefits. And since the prison is a social system that has been created by humans, is operated by humans and serves humanity, it is completely under our control. Therefore, even minor modifications to the prison's environment, given time, can reduce or altogether eliminate the effects of chaos, ensuring that the prison will become more effective at breaking the crime cycle.

In the next chapter the big bang and the expansion of the universe are considered. These events are compared to the prison's development and our growing use of incarceration as a formal sanction. It is within this framework that the prison's future is explored with two possibilities being identified - the first possibility is continued expansion and growth, whereas the second is contraction that results in declining prison populations. Based upon physical laws, if contraction were to occur, the prison's ability to help break the crime cycle would be dramatically improved through the liberation of energy and resources.

HIGHLIGHTS

- Chaos theories, whether they are biologically, mathematically or philosophically oriented, share a set of common principles.
- Chaos theories are among the most complex theories that we have yet encountered.
- The term chaos suggests that events are occurring in a disordered, haphazard and unpredictable fashion.
- Chaos is always perceived as undesirable since it results in inconsistent and unpredictable outcomes.
- Chaos always negatively impacts a system's operations, making ongoing performance evaluations increasingly necessary.
- The prison's effectiveness can only be determined by considering recidivism rates since they are the only measure by which the prison's actions and outcomes can be comprehensively assessed.
- Systems are highly sensitive to the conditions in which they operate. Small changes to an environment can create widely divergent outcomes.
- Social systems are affected by environmental conditions including, at the individual level, experience, emotion, cognitive development and amenability. At the institutional level those environmental factors that can affect operations include philosophical orientation, access to appropriate personnel and economic realities.
- Factors, including politics, can affect both individual and institutional behaviors and their associated outcomes.
- A system's actions and its associated outcomes may become more chaotic and less predictable over time.
- As a system operates and as greater amounts of time pass, the opportunity for environmental condition to affect operations increase.
- Within the prison system, chaos can be defined as a disjunction that exists between the expectations of the taxpaying public and the actual effects that stem from imprisonment.

- Any social system plagued by chaos will produce outcomes that are not aligned with the public's expectation or its welfare.

- A chaotic prison system will, at the individual level, fail to rehabilitate the inmate and at the institutional level will be reflected in disordered and ineffective operations.

- A properly functioning prison system will produce low recidivism rates - a chaotic prison system will be plagued by exceptionally high recidivism rates.

- Recidivism is the only measure by which the prison's short and long-term benefits to society can be evaluated - recidivism rates also reveal the degree of chaos present within our prisons.

- This observation is worth repeating - a system's actions and its corresponding outcomes are directly linked to internal and external conditions as well as the length of time that the system has been in operation.

- A system's sensitivity to environmental conditions and the ability of these conditions to produce unpredictable outcomes is often referred to as the "butterfly effect".

- The phrase "butterfly effect" appeared in a paper authored by MIT professor Edward Lorenz.

- A young system is often more predictable than an aged system.

- Over time, predictability is adversely affected as environmental conditions are dispersed throughout a system. Time and this dispersal exponentially increase the collective ability of these conditions to affect outcome.

- Vital to all chaos perspectives is recognition that even small changes in the conditions of a system can have huge impacts on outcome.

- Modern institutions are increasingly being viewed as complex social systems that share many characteristics in common with those systems found within the natural realm.

- All systems whether they are of the natural or social variety are subject to internal and external forces that may contribute to a chaotic state.

- Chaos is an inability or even an outright refusal by prison officials to utilize resources to break the crime cycle.

- Chaos is reflected in the distance that the prison has placed between itself and its traditional objective of offender rehabilitation.

- Prison officials are increasingly unable to delineate the benefits associated with imprisonment (beyond incapacitation).

- The taxpayer expects imprisonment to break the crime cycle yet the contemporary prison appears to be little more than a human warehouse.

- Opponents of treatment effectively seized upon isolated events of inmate violence as evidence that the prison should eliminate all non-essential services with education, training and therapy being considered "non-essential".

- The confusion caused by urging the prison to break from its traditional objectives was both a symptom and a producer of chaos.

- An increase in the frequency of prison riots during the latter part of the twentieth century was not itself considered a result of the "nothing works" movement.

- Opponents of treatment sought to create a prison system whereby the effects of incarceration on the inmate population would be determined entirely by fate. As such, officials would no longer seek to control the prison's culture but would instead, by their acquiescence, effectively relinquish much of their control to inmate leadership.

- Both liberals and conservatives widely embraced an anti-treatment approach. Since treatment lacked support from either political party, an anti-treatment perspective gained legitimacy.

- An anti-treatment perspective was effectively used to strip the prison of its humanity, ushering in a chaotic era in which a cold, detached and sterile approach came to dominate.

- Changes in political perspectives, though they started small, gained considerable momentum over time and much like our butterfly, have created a major disturbance in the correctional environment.

- The effects of chaos are similar regardless of whether a system is of the natural or social variety.

- Our inability to predict the weather is due to the effect of environmental variables on the development of atmospheric conditions. Any single environmental variable (including pressure, temperature and humidity) can produce changes in weather patterns, and when these variables exert their collective influence by combining, predictions become much less accurate.

- Time gives variables an opportunity to combine and recombine in unique ways with each of these permutations having a differing effect on outcome.

- Chaos within a social system is evidenced in outcomes that often run contrary to the health and wellbeing of society.

- While we remain confident that our hypothetical pendulum's bob will reverse its current direction, we are not able to determine when, to what degree or under what circumstances this may occur.

- Rehabilitation reduces the effects of chaos - and if accomplished on a large scale, would result in a lowering of crime rates and correctional expenditures.

QUESTIONS

1). What is chaos? What is the relationship between chaos theory and the weather? Within a social context, is it fair to suggest that chaos is an inability or even an outright refusal by prison officials to utilize resources to break the crime cycle? Explain.

2). A system's actions and its associated outcomes may become more chaotic and less predictable over time. Why?

3). Does recidivism accurately measure the degree of chaos within the prison? Do other measures exist? If so, what are they? Explain.

4). What is the butterfly effect? How does it apply to prison operations? What events are responsible for creating recent disturbances in the correctional environment? Explain.

5). It was noted that perceptions, beliefs, opinions and interactions often produce a great deal of bias, misinformation, distortions of fact and error. Does this affect the prison's operations and ideology? Explain. Could this impede the prison's ability to break the crime cycle? Explain.

6). Do you believe that social events/activities are cyclical in nature? Explain. Is it possible that with each swing of our pendulum's bob, periods marked by punitive ideology grow increasingly longer in duration while periods marked by a pro-treatment rationale become increasingly shorter? Why? What does this possibility suggest for the future of the prison? Explain.

7). How have changes in political perceptions about inmates affected the prison? How have they affected the inmate? In your opinion, were these changes foreseeable? Explain.

CHAPTER SEVEN
Applying Humanized Physics to Penology: Parallels between the Physical and Social Realms

Is it true that all things that expand eventually contract? Perhaps...

As socio-physicists, we entertain the possibility that there may be a set of universal laws that govern both the physical and social realms. As such, the explanatory and predictive ability of any specific discipline will increase when knowledge from multiple fields is combined. If we are to improve the human condition, we must cross the lines that have traditionally separated the sciences. An interdisciplinary approach that applies physical laws to the social realm promises to provide an increased understanding of human behavior.

In previous chapters it was concluded that the prison is gravitating toward a lower energy state. It was surmised that since rehabilitation is more energy dependent than are other penal objectives, contemporary efforts to curtail treatment reflect a decrease in free or available energies. Furthermore, it appears that the prison is moving toward an increased level of entropy and chaos as indicated by rising recidivism rates among ex-inmates. And finally, it was observed that when an object or system gains or loses mass, its behavior is affected. A prison's mass is equivalent to the size of its inmate population and as this population has risen, the prison has become less treatment oriented.

There is an undeniable value in comparing the prison to an atom's nucleus with each being visualized as the unifying force through which interactions occur. The proton can be compared to those inmates displaying a favorable or positive attitude toward treatment, whereas the electron can be compared to those inmates displaying an unfavorable or negative attitude toward treatment. This approach (reminiscent of Niels Bohr, a Nobel physicist) was endorsed by Richard Feynman (another Nobel physicist) who asserted that the actions of all living things can be explained once we realize that they are made up of atoms acting in accordance with the laws of physics. It was also observed that when opposite charges (or orientations) exist within a system, energy tends to flow in one direction - from a negative toward a positive state. If energy and peer influence are comparable, and if particles and prisoners are similar, then negatively oriented inmates are having a detrimental influence on those with a positive orientation. Therefore, the current practice of housing amenable and nonamenable inmates within a common facility would seem to perpetuate criminality and lead to unnecessarily high recidivism rates. To break this cycle, an insulator was proposed to protect amenable inmates from the corrupting effects of negativity.

The approaches taken herein reveal the conceptual and theoretical abilities of physics to provide insight into the complexities of social phenomena. Utilizing socio-physics in the present fashion requires a determination to be made about whether parallels exist between the natural and social realms and to what extent physics is able to provide insight into human behavior. The great educational philosopher Edwin Slosson, when studying America's universities, suggested that all institutions of higher learning create a Department of Humanized Physics. While the intricacies of Slosson's proposal have been lost to posterity, he was thoroughly versed in the natural sciences and was clearly a proponent of interdisciplinary cooperation especially when it involved using physics to study the human condition. Furthermore, John Trumpbour (an educational historian), when writing about scientific ideologies, observed that most fields including philosophy, are indebted to the advancements in thought brought about by Newtonian physics. In fact, academicians have long sought to discover a set of laws that unify the physical and social sciences.

In the following pages, the big bang is considered the natural equivalent to the creation of America's prison system since each is a genesis event. Similarly, the expansion of the universe is considered a natural parallel to the expanded use of incarceration since each denotes an inflationary event. While we refrain from suggesting that parallels always exist between the physical and social realms, those that do exist promise to provide increased insight into human behavior. And while the approach taken within this chapter is admittedly unorthodox, it nonetheless permits us to think outside the box. This proves beneficial if one believes, as did Feynman, that social phenomena are more difficult to understand than are natural phenomena. The quest for knowledge using socio-physics is pertinent to penologists since few institutions have a greater impact on human behavior or public safety than the prison. To that end, the big bang and cosmic inflation were selected for inclusion for three reasons. First, each is easily recognizable. In fact, it is difficult to imagine an adult who hasn't encountered theories related to these events. Secondly, no single occurrence has resulted in greater scientific conjecture and exploration than has the origins of our existence. And finally, this effort pays homage to U.S. Supreme Court Judge William Paterson (1795) who compared the planetary and social realms - the first recorded comparison of its kind by a criminal justice official.

The Big Bang and Inflation

Most people have wondered about the birth of the universe. Respective questions include, "How was the Earth created?" and "Where did all this stuff come from?" These and similar questions are the products of healthy and inquisitive minds. For example, it is quite common for children to ask questions about where the stars and planets came from, and by default, where "we" come from. While humankind has sought answers to the secrets of creation for millennia, it wasn't until the early twentieth century that science had advanced to the point where natural phenomena could be explained through systematic observation, the use of testable hypotheses and the development of theory. One early and widely accepted explanation for the existence of the universe was the Steady State Theory. This theory ignored questions about the genesis of the universe and instead held that it has always and will always exist. In essence, the universe had no beginning and will have no end. Stephen Hawking, an internationally renowned physicist, refers to this theory as the "it just is" conjecture. However, scientific advancements in physics, cosmology and astronomy increasingly began to challenge the notion of a static universe. As early as 1912, scientists witnessed celestial objects moving away from Earth. In fact, it appeared that the stars and planets were being pushed along by some unseen force. This observation left scientists temporarily unsure of how to interpret their observations. Then in 1927, Georges Lemaitre, a Roman Catholic priest and amateur physicist, suggested that the entire universe was expanding. His theory implied that at some earlier time, all matter was compressed into an inconceivably small point of infinite density and temperature called a singularity. Furthermore, he reasoned that it would have taken an explosive event to scatter this matter and create space itself. Cosmic inflation, as it is now called, refers to the exponential growth of the early universe, with expansion continuing even today. Paul Dirac (Nobel physicist) believed that this discovery and its implications may ultimately provide insight into the complexities of nature itself.

During a 1949 radio broadcast, Fred Hoyle an English astronomer and an outspoken proponent of the Steady State Theory, coined the expression "big bang". He used this phrase to refer sarcastically to Lemaitre's suggestion concerning the universe's origin. Despite his open opposition to Lemaitre, other scientists including George Gamow, Ralph Alpher and Robert Herman proceeded to develop the Big Bang Theory. These scientists, and others, predicted that an explosion of such enormity would have produced residual radiation that should still be detectable today, even though it occurred an estimated 13.7 billion years ago. And in fact, this radiation was discovered in 1964 by Arno Penzias and Robert Wilson (Bell Laboratories) earning each of them a Nobel Prize. Scientific models based on the Big Bang Theory suggest that the universe will follow one of these paths:

- it will continue to expand, or
- it will continue to expand (for another few billion years) but will eventually contract and return to a point of singularity, or
- it will undergo a never-ending series of expansions and contractions.

While the first possibility lends itself to speculation about the ultimate fate of the universe, it is the second and third possibilities that prove valuable to the present effort. Whether the universe is engaged in a continuous cycle of expansion and contraction remains debatable, what is of particular interest is that two of these possibilities suggest that expansion is inevitably followed by contraction. Therefore, for all intents and purposes, we will treat the second and third possibilities as a single prospect.

Operating under the premise that expansion is clear and compelling evidence of a big bang event, we should recognize that the effects of expansion are numerous and potentially catastrophic. As the universe was created, and as matter was propelled outward from its point of origin, energy began to dissipate, being spread ever more thinly. Moreover, as energy was converted into matter, its availability decreased even further. And finally, expansion leads to entropy. Entropy as you may recall is the inability of energy to be used effectively or to be transformed from one of its various forms (i.e. heat, light, and electricity) into another form. We refer to these effects as the detriments of expansion because they create a state of progressive decline. For example, as the universe continues to expand, its temperature (a measure of its free energy content) will decrease, eventually subjecting it to heat death. Heat death denotes the process by which the energy content of the universe dissipates to such an extent that its temperature reaches absolute zero. In essence, as energy is spread ever more thinly, and as entropy progresses, the universe will grow increasingly cold and dark.

While the ultimate fate of the universe remains unknown, expansion may have its limits. The General Theory of Relativity permits both the expansion and contraction of space, each of which is controlled by gravity, a force that attracts all objects toward one another. Gravity is the force that will pull this book downward, should you let it slip from your hands or fall from your desk. Respective computer modeling, based upon scientific data, suggests that expansion may eventually slow to the point where the universe begins to contract. However, this possibility is dependent upon whether enough matter exists in the universe for its collective gravitational effect to result in a form of cosmic elasticity. Cosmic elasticity can be visualized as being similar to the resistance that is encountered when one stretches a rubber band, suggesting that the universe may eventually snap back, returning to its original state. While this potentiality is often referred to as the "big crunch" we prefer to call it the "rubber band effect". If this occurs, a point of singularity would again be achieved, allowing the universe's energy, temperature and denseness to eventually return to their pre-inflationary levels. Think of it this way, if the universe was to shrink, it would grow increasingly hot and dense with its energy content being concentrated into an ever decreasing area. This process would continue until the moment of another big bang. Since expansion is predicted to continue for at least another ten billion years, the cycle of expansion, contraction and rebirth may take untold millennia.

Social Parallel

Any parallel existing between the big bang and the creation of America's prison system begins with the establishment of the Walnut Street Jail (1773). This facility served as both a jail and prison for the city of Philadelphia and is recognized as our earliest correctional institution of significance. While much of its history has been lost, it was originally a small and densely populated facility. Due to its modest size, its limited capacity quickly proved inadequate. Officials soon took notice and expanded it in 1790. This increased its total capacity to perhaps 200 inmates, yet even its enlarged size proved inadequate. In response, the Pennsylvania legislature authorized the construction of two additional facilities - Western Penitentiary in Pittsburgh and Eastern Penitentiary in Philadelphia. Within a few decades, Pennsylvania's prison population reached nearly 2,000 inmates. The growth of our nation's inmate population has continued ever since. For example, prison populations during the 1900s increased, at times, by nearly 10,000 inmates per year and as the end of the twentieth century neared, the nation's prisons were experiencing a net gain of nearly 40,000 inmates per year. This expansion suggests that a major shift has occurred in our approach to crime and punishment.

While it is inherently difficult to offer generalizations about prevailing ideologies, it is nonetheless necessary to the present undertaking. When we consider each decade since 1930 and compare its prevailing political ideology (favoring either punishment or rehabilitation) to the size of its inmate population, it becomes apparent that during eras characterized by a punitive political ideology, both the number of prisons and inmates increased. Similarly, during those eras characterized by a treatment ideology, expansion slowed and a period of contraction usually resulted (the most recent period of contraction occurred from 1960 - 70). While poorly kept records and inconsistent data make it difficult to trace the history of the prison with precision, evidence suggests that there have been numerous periods in which the prison has expanded and then contracted. Further comparisons between the big bang, inflation and incarceration require a determination to be made about the level of energy and entropy present within the contemporary prison.

Expansion and Contraction

In previous chapters, the following observations were offered:

- energy flows from a state of excitement toward a state of rest,
- the amount of energy within the prison varies but tends to dissipate over time,
- the prison's ability to promote public safety (on a long-term basis) tends to decrease over time,
- fluctuations in the prison's mass and/or energy levels produce corresponding changes in behavior, and
- the prison's operating ideology, whether it favors punishment or rehabilitation, will remain unchanged unless forced to act otherwise.

These observations suggest that the prison is governed by laws that have counterparts within the natural sciences. To determine how these counterparts apply, one must begin by evaluating the amount of energy present within the contemporary prison, and the most logical way to do this is through an assessment of its involvement in treatment. Since offender rehabilitation is the most energy dependent objective of the prison, its pursuit requires a significant outlay of resources. It is this outlay (or lack thereof) that makes such an assessment possible. Similarly, the only way to determine whether energy is being used effectively is to determine the prison's current level of entropy by considering the recidivism rates of its former inmates.

To assess rehabilitation, we must recognize that it has long been the guiding operational philosophy of our prison system. It was sanctioned by the puritanical principles of forgiveness and salvation, though at times its pursuit was admittedly inhumane. As early as the sixteenth century, offender rehabilitation was viewed as critical for the advancement and continuing welfare of society. Its prominence within penology has repeatedly been affirmed by political and correctional leaders. But as the 1970s approached, debate about its achievability became a politicized topic partly due to the growing destructiveness, magnitude and frequency of prison riots. The impact that these events had on the American psyche was profound, creating the perception that our nation's prisons were wholly ineffective at facilitating offender reform. It was increasingly argued that the prison should simply house inmates as cheaply as possible, providing few programs and provisions. The political machinery came to view treatment as being financially wasteful and ideologically unsound. To this end, resources for treatment were significantly curtailed.

The current ideology that devalues rehabilitation while promoting wholesale incarceration is contributing to the prison's increased mass. When the prison gains or loses mass, its energy levels fluctuate. As the prison's mass has increased, a rerouting of energy has become necessary to meet the needs of a large and growing inmate population. This has led to additional decreases in treatment initiatives, which is significant since these programs (which include educational, vocational and counseling services) appear to be functioning as makeshift batteries from which needed energy and resources are being drawn. Thus, many treatment programs have been downgraded or eliminated with their previously earmarked resources being used to support the immediate needs of a large inmate population.

Gravity and Rehabilitation

Consider gravity and an interest in rehabilitation to be functional equivalents since each can be described as an attracting force. While gravity can be visualized as a force that exists between objects, interest or what we call social gravity can be visualized as a force that binds individuals and groups to a common or shared objective. In the case of rehabilitation, correctional personnel have historically sought to promote pro-social attitudes, impart knowledge and assist offenders in developing those skills necessary for meaningful citizenship. This transaction has required the interest and cooperation of all parties and when successfully achieved, it maximized the constructive aspects of incarceration, thereby minimizing recidivism rates. When a shared interest in treatment is strong, therapeutic programs flourish, leading to reduced recidivism rates. Stated somewhat differently, a broad and pervasive interest in offender rehabilitation, regardless of why it exists, promotes treatment and encourages contraction. Similarly, contraction, regardless of why it begins, liberates energy that can then be used to promote rehabilitation. In essence, if an interest in rehabilitation is sufficiently strong, expansion will slow to the point where the prison will begin to contract. Were this to occur, the number of inmates and prisons would decrease, perhaps returning to their pre-expansion (pre-1980s) level. This process once began, would likely feed upon itself, picking up momentum and support as it progresses. As you may have already anticipated, this event would be the social equivalent of the rubber band effect.

When considering incarceration rates since 1890, it becomes obvious that contraction tends to be relatively short in duration (usually lasting about 10 years), whereas periods of expansion tend to be much longer (lasting about 40 years). Since the most recent period of expansion began in 1970 (gaining incredible speed in the early 1980s), it appears that we are now overdue for a contraction event. While current signs suggest that expansion may be slowing, it is too early to determine whether the overall size of the inmate population will be affected. Interestingly enough, if the corrections system were to experience a contraction event similar to the one that occurred from 1960 - 70 (an approximate decrease of 12% in the inmate population), the number of inmates (both in our jails and prisons) would shrink by about 300,000 individuals. This would save about $7.5 billion per year (using a conservative figure of $25,000 per year to house an inmate).

If the big bang and inflation are comparable to the creation and expansion of America's prisons, then it stands to reason that during contraction events, those observations previously offered about the prison would work in reverse. For example, during periods of contraction:

- energy levels within the prison would gradually move toward the higher end of the energy spectrum, resulting in an increase in the number and diversity of treatment programs offered as well as in the intensity by which rehabilitation would be pursued,
- rising energy levels would result in decreased entropy as evidenced by the prison's growing efforts at, and ultimate effectiveness in, achieving offender reform, and
- energy levels would peak just prior to the commencement of yet another expansion event.

It is likely that the causes producing the next contraction event will be numerous and multifaceted and may result from political and/or economic changes, an official recognition that mass incarceration proves counterproductive to public safety, or the acknowledgement that incarceration without treatment is socially irresponsible. Whatever the reason or reasons may be, contraction will likely occur within the near future and may help return some ideological balance (albeit temporarily) to a system that has increasingly proven itself ineffective and costly. It is important to realize that by its very nature, contemporary punishment demands incremental intensification. Over time, this results in the unchecked expansion and amplification of punitive pursuits. The harshest punishment currently available (execution notwithstanding) is imprisonment, suggesting that in the absence of a contraction event, the use of the prison will remain a popular sanction with future expansion being both likely and significant.

At the cosmic level, expansion can be equated to coldness, entropy and death. Contraction, on the other hand, is analogous to heat and an abundance of energy. If we were to apply this same observation to the prison, we would conclude that its expansion has similarly resulted in a form of institutional coldness that has rendered it ineffective at promoting the long-term interests of society. Conversely, contraction would increase the prison's energy levels and its ability to promote offender reform. In essence, contraction would result in a partial or complete reversal of the detriments of expansion. If social gravity and physical gravity are equivalents, and if gravity plays a large role in producing a contraction event, then the next contraction event for the prison may be brought about by a growing interest in rehabilitation and a desire to reduce crime and recidivism. It is simply too early to determine whether an interest in rehabilitation will lead to a contraction event or whether a contraction event (perhaps prompted by growing financial shortcomings) will contribute to an increased interest in the long-term benefits associated with rehabilitation.

Conclusion

Knowing that we may be approaching a contraction event serves to notify correctional practitioners and penologists alike, that they should begin to prepare. While past contraction events have been short in duration, their longevity might be increased through a more complete understanding of historical trends and the intelligent and deliberate application of penal theory. Overall, we still know little about human and institutional behavior. While the fields of psychology, sociology and organizational management offer insight, it would prove beneficial for all scholars to consider the possibility that natural laws and processes can and do shed light on human behavior. Penologists should increasingly turn their attention toward the study of energy flow, its relationship to the promotion of public safety, and how entropy, expansion, contraction and ideology all affect operational effectiveness.

In the next chapter consideration is given to prison specialization and how specialized correctional institutions can effectively promote rehabilitation. This includes a review of the foundations for specialization as well as the role that inmate amenability plays within treatment processes. In addition to inmate amenability, prison administrators are seen as ignoring their responsibility to promote pro-social values by permitting a culture of opposition to flourish among inmate populations.

HIGHLIGHTS

- A discipline's ability to explain and predict increases when knowledge from multiple fields is considered.
- If we are to improve the human condition we must cross those lines that have traditionally separated the sciences.
- Rehabilitation is a proactive pursuit that is more energy-dependent than are the prison's other objectives.
- The contemporary movement to curtail treatment suggests that the amount of energy available within the prison is decreasing.
- A prison's mass is equivalent to the size of its inmate population and as this population has risen, the prison's actions have become less treatment oriented.
- Most fields including philosophy are indebted to the advancements in thought brought about by Newtonian physics.
- Few institutions have a greater impact on public safety than the prison.
- It wasn't until the early twentieth century that science had advanced to the point where natural phenomena were being explained through systematic observation, the use of hypotheses and the development of theory.
- Steady State Theory holds that the universe has always and will always exist.
- As early as 1912, scientists witnessed celestial objects moving away from Earth, leaving them temporarily unsure of how to interpret their observations.
- In 1927, Georges Lemaitre, a Roman Catholic priest and amateur physicist suggested that the entire universe was expanding.
- Fred Hoyle, an English astronomer, sarcastically coined the phrase *big bang* to refer to the proposition that the universe's expansion began with an explosion.
- The effects of expansion are potentially catastrophic.

- Entropy is the inability of energy to be used effectively or to be transformed from one of its various forms into another.

- Heat death denotes the process by which the universe's energy dissipates to such an extent that its temperature reaches absolute zero.

- The expansion of the universe may eventually slow to the point where it begins to contract.

- The phrase *cosmic elasticity* refers to the possibility that the universe may eventually snap back, returning to its original state.

- Any parallel between the big bang and the creation of America's prison system begins with the establishment of the Walnut Street Jail, our nation's earliest correctional institution of significance.

- By the end of the twentieth century, our nation's prisons were experiencing a net gain of approximately 40,000 inmates per year.

- The probability that a citizen will be incarcerated during his/her lifetime has tripled in the past four decades, suggesting that a major shift has occurred in America's political ideology and penal practices.

- When we consider each decade since 1930 and compare its prevailing political ideology to the size of its inmate population, it becomes apparent that during eras characterized by a punitive rational, both the number of prisons and inmates increased. However, during those eras characterized by a treatment ideology, expansion slowed and during at least one decade (1960 - 70) a period of contraction resulted.

- While poorly kept records and inconsistent data make it difficult to trace the history of the prison with precision, evidence suggests that there have been numerous periods in which the prison has expanded and then contracted.

- To determine the effects of entropy on the prison, one must measure the amount of energy present within the contemporary correctional institution, and the most logical way to do this is through an assessment of its involvement (or lack thereof) in treatment.

- The only way to measure the prison's current level of entropy as defined by its ability to apply energy in an efficient and effective manner is to consider the recidivism rates of its former inmates.

- In the absence of the humanizing effects associated with treatment, the prison's environment has steadily deteriorated.
- Ninety-percent of all citizens support treatment for inmates.
- The word *corrections* suggests that rehabilitation remains an objective of the prison even if its pursuit has been curtailed.
- It is important to recognize that the current ideology which promotes incarceration strictly as a punitive measure has contributed to the prison's increased mass.
- When the prison gains or loses mass, its energy levels fluctuate.
- Those therapeutic programs that are still in existence are functioning as makeshift batteries from which needed energy and resources are being drawn.
- Consider gravity and an interest in rehabilitation to be functional equivalents since each can be described as an attracting force.
- While gravity can be visualized as a force that exists between objects, social gravity can be visualized as a force that binds individuals or groups to a common or shared objective.
- A reduction in both the number of inmates and prisons would be the social equivalent of the *rubber band effect.*
- Contraction within the prison tends to be relatively short (usually lasting about 10 years), whereas periods of expansion tend to be much longer (lasting about 40 years).
- While prison admissions are slowing, commitments continue to outnumber releases.
- If the corrections system were to experience a contraction event similar to the one that occurred from 1960 - 1970, the number of jail and prison inmates would shrink by nearly 300,000 individuals, saving approximately $7.5 billion annually.
- The causes of the next contraction event will likely be numerous and multifaceted and may result from political and/or economic changes, an official recognition that wholesale incarceration is counterproductive to

public safety, or the acknowledgement that incarceration without treatment is socially irresponsible.

- By their very nature, contemporary forms of correctional intervention demand incremental intensification resulting in the unchecked expansion and amplification of punitive pursuits.

- At the cosmic level, expansion is equivalent to coldness, entropy and death, while contraction is analogous to heat and an abundance of energy. If we were to apply this same observation to the prison, we would conclude that its expansion has similarly resulted in a form of institutional coldness that renders it ineffective at promoting the long-term interest of society. Conversely, contraction would increase the prison's energy levels and its ability to promote offender reform.

QUESTIONS

1). How does mass affect both physical and social processes? Explain.

2). Scientific models based on the Big Bang Theory suggest that the universe may be engaged in a series of expansion and contraction events. Are there parallels between these models and the actions of the prison? Explain.

3). What role does energy play within the prison? Do energy levels in social systems tend to dissipate over time? Explain. What does your response suggest for future prison operations and offender rehabilitation?

4). The observation was made that existing treatment programs are currently being used as makeshift batteries from which energy and resources are being drawn. Is it possible that the continued existence of these programs is intended to satisfy a public demand for treatment, but in reality exist only to serve the short-term purposes of the prison? Explain.

5). Is it probable that the prison will experience a contraction event within the next few years? Explain.

6). Is rehabilitation the most energy dependent objective of the prison? Explain.

7). What is meant by the term social gravity? What role, if any, would it play in bringing about a contraction event?

8). Do punitive pursuits demand incremental intensification? Base your response on the recent use of the prison as a criminal sanction.

CHAPTER EIGHT
Prison Specialization and Offender Amenability

Specialization creates the knowledge, skills and practices necessary to break the crime cycle.

While a get tough approach to crime remains politically popular, questions persist about the extent to which it actually promotes public safety. This uncertainty is leading some penologists to consider alternative ways to meet this objective. In doing so, they are demonstrating to future penologists the value of innovative, creative and progressive thinking. One creative approach to incarceration that is worthy of our consideration is prison specialization. Proponents of specialization recognize that there are generally two groups of inmates, those who are amenable to therapeutic intervention (protons) and those who resist such measures (electrons). Under respective proposals, prisons would separate the amenable inmate from the nonamenable inmate population, thereby minimizing the likelihood for contact. The purpose of this practice is to safeguard the integrity of treatment by shielding amenable inmates from the negative influence of those who may impede rehabilitation.

Let us preface this chapter by stating that similar to the previous chapters it is for all intents and purposes conceptual in nature. However, we do mention research that we have informally conducted. This research is based primarily on opportunistic interviews conducted over the past decade. The specific purpose of this chapter is to introduce readers to an alternative to traditional inmate classification processes by providing insights obtained from those individuals who are intimately familiar with this approach. These individuals include those who are confined within the prison's walls as well as prison staff.

As contemporary penologists with access to a great amount of scholarship, we find that it is inescapably obvious that few advancements have been suggested, developed or implemented in the area of inmate classification. Classification is the process of determining an inmate's security and treatment needs. All jurisdictions mandate classification at least annually; however, most inmates undergo the classification process more often, usually due to changes in housing, job assignment or institutional transfer (each requires a reassessment of one's classification status). Traditionally, inmates were given a security rating of maximum, medium or minimum. Of course, this determination was based on an inmate's criminal record, propensity toward violence and factors such as gang affiliation. While jurisdictions nationwide have adopted new security ratings that often designate inmates as being Level I through Level V offenders, with each level representing an increase or decrease in danger, all approaches reflect the risks associated with a particular inmate.

Historically, an inmate's security rating was only half the equation. Each inmate was also given an institutional treatment plan based on an assessment of his or her needs. Once an assessment was completed, an appropriate form of intervention could then be designed and implemented. Typical forms of intervention included provisions for educational, vocational and counseling services. While security designations have stood the test of time, treatment plans have increasingly become less integral to the prison's operations. This is due to changes in political and penal practices, the prison's inability to provide services to such a large inmate population and the financial need to reduce or eliminate all non-essential expenditures.

The Problem

The prison has traditionally been reluctant to adopt new and innovative ideas. This hesitancy is more pronounced today than ever before, enslaving the prison to its own traditions. The prison has, to a greater extent than other institutions, come to rely more heavily on rote activity than innovative practice. Its failure to invest in more progressive approaches has hindered its ability to reform inmates and promote public safety. In fact, one might argue that since correctional officials first began to classify and separate inmates based on sex, age and offense, few similar advances have been implemented. Consider if you will that even the earliest depictions of the prison differ remarkably little from those of today. Put simply, the prison exhibits a timelessness that is seldom found elsewhere.

As timeless as the prison may be, inquisitive researchers continue to seek information about its operations and the effects of incarceration from those who know it best. Over an eighteen-year period between 1990 and 1992, 1994 and 1997, and 2002 to the present, we spoke with inmates, ex-inmates and staff of four different state correctional systems; two in the Midwest, one in the Southwest, and one in the Southeast. We conducted interviews with nearly 300 individuals. These interviews were unstructured, opportunistic and informal in nature. Most of the interviewees were offenders (80%) with sentences ranging from 18 months to life without parole. Correctional employees made up the remaining 20 percent and included new staff as well as those with careers exceeding two decades. Employees included representatives from security, classification, treatment and administrative services. All interviewees were asked open-ended questions about the prison's objectives, asked to rank these objectives by perceived importance, and offer observations about change within the prison. The objectives that respondents collectively identified and were then asked to rank by their importance included incapacitation, retribution, deterrence and rehabilitation. Nearly 90% of all participants identified rehabilitation as the most important objective of the prison. Similarly, almost an identical number of participants indicated that inmate reform is currently given little attention by the prison's officials. A consistency in these statements emerged with approximately 92% indicating that the prison has changed little during their confinement or employment.

As interviews were conducted, one administrator provided us with several items pertaining to the early prison. Among these items was the *Handbook on Classification in Correctional Institutions* (referred to hereafter as the *Handbook*) published in 1947 by the American Prison Association (now known as the American Correctional Association) and republished in 1965. Since its publication, it has proven to be a valuable resource. The *Handbook* is a small and unassuming work that has served for many years as the only national source of information available on inmate classification and treatment. While seventy years have passed since its initial publication, its authors (30 in all) proclaimed offender reform a necessary pursuit of the prison for the benefit of both the inmate and society. In addition to advocating changes to classification processes, several of these penologists also called for the creation of specialized prisons. Noted penologist Howard Gill (an expert on inmate classification and treatment) suggested that society might be spared the personal, social and financial costs associated with repeated criminality if specialized prisons were created. While many classification manuals have appeared since the *Handbook* was first published, none have so clearly advocated or outlined the benefits of specialization. Before we consider prison specialization in greater detail, ponder the following excerpt (as it appears in the *Handbook*) which details the belief that the public's interest can best be served through inmate reform:

> The public's welfare can best be protected by returning as many prisoners as possible to the community, fitted educationally and vocationally, in physical and mental health and through changed attitudes and ideals, to take their places as law abiding citizens. The necessity for a program, which will have a constructive effect upon prisoners, is based upon the

> inescapable fact that over 95% of all prisoners committed to prison are sooner or later returned to the community. The prison has the grave responsibility of determining whether they shall be returned less criminally inclined or with criminal attitudes more fixed and with criminal abilities more fully developed.

The observations that appear within this statement contain a profound logic - the necessity for prison officials to challenge those attitudes and actions (of either inmates or staff) that perpetuate criminality. In essence, the prison must be a proactive institution that embraces its role as a producer of public safety. When statements of this nature are considered, it becomes evident that early penologists were convinced that the prison must adhere to the highest expectations and standards possible. By doing so its ability to promote the public's safety would be enhanced.

The Solution

Any proposal calling for the establishment of specialized prisons must be historically based in order to be perceived as legitimate. And in fact, prison specialization dates to the thirteenth century. It was then that correctional officials in London began to experiment with specialized prisons as part and parcel of their normal practice. While little scholarship exists to tell us about the operational specifics of these early institutions, those records that do exist suggest that each specialized prison held a different type of offender. For example, some of these institutions housed less serious and less experienced offenders while others housed more serious, chronic and hardened offenders. While a comprehensive description of these early institutions is lacking, a more complete accounting exists with regard to related practices that emerged in North America.

In North America, the groundwork for specialization dates to the eighteenth century. During that time, several important events took place. First, a group of progressive penal thinkers met at the home of Benjamin Franklin to develop an ideology for prison operations. At this meeting, ideas about treatment and inmate amenability began to emerge. This meeting represents the earliest recorded affirmation of rehabilitation as an official American penal objective. Shortly thereafter, officials of the Walnut Street Jail put many of these ideas into practice. The Walnut Street Jail, which we have previously mentioned, is widely considered the first American prison to implement a classification process designed to promote inmate reform. But why did its officials adopt such an approach? This is a reasonable question given previous statements pertaining to the paralyzing effects of tradition on prison operations. Yet, the answer is simple. Early American prisons had not yet created their own traditions and therefore, officials felt much freer to experiment than do their contemporary counterparts. Furthermore, these innovative actions were the result of public pressure. These actions occurred at the urging of the Philadelphia Society for Alleviating the Miseries of Public Prisons. This group of concerned citizens convinced officials to separate inmates based on sex, age and perceived dangerousness. Prior to their involvement, all inmates regardless of these characteristics were housed in the same facility where contact occurred freely. As you can imagine, victimization of weaker and less assertive inmates was common. This early decision to classify and separate inmates was a significant step in the evolution of the prison. It solidified the belief that an offender's attributes must be considered when determining his/her classification status and housing assignment. However, since officials stopped short of separating inmates based on amenability, prison specialization was never implemented to the extent advocated herein.

Now let's leap ahead to modernity where specialization is still occasionally discussed. Generally speaking, supporters of specialization believe that inmates can be separated into two groups. These groups consist of those with the desire and capacity to undergo treatment (considered amenable) and conversely those who are opposed to treatment (considered nonamenable). A third category is also occasionally mentioned and includes those inmates who exhibit emotional or mental impediments that make their full participation in treatment difficult or impossible. For simplicity's sake, we shall disregard this latter group. Thus, specialization requires a determination to be made about the amenability of each particular inmate. This determination would then serve as the basis for an offender's institutional placement. Of course, amenable inmates would be housed in units or prisons designed to meet their specific needs. Nonamenable inmates would be housed in separate institutions (or separate areas within the same institution) where contact with the amenable population would not occur. This separation should not be confused with the traditional practice of segregating inmates for disciplinary purposes. Instead, it is preventative in nature, and while a majority of the nonamenable inmate population is not openly defiant or confrontational, most do have negative views about correctional intervention that challenges authority, disrupts operations, and corrupts those inmates who are susceptible to subtle or overt influence.

As you can see, specialization runs counter to the contemporary practice of housing amenable and nonamenable inmates within the same prisons. For example, Gill declared our current approach to inmate classification a poor practice that permits intermingling to occur between these two groups. The foundation for prison specialization rests firmly upon the following assertions:

- a great deal of diversity exists within the inmate population,
- there are inmates who desire treatment (amenables) as well as those who oppose it (nonamenables),
- it must be determined into which group each inmate belongs,
- members of these two groups should be housed separately, just as we now separate female inmates from their male counterparts and juveniles from adult inmates,
- the separation of these two groups requires that each prison (or area thereof) be equipped to deal with either the amenable or nonamenable inmate but not both,

- separating members of these two groups protects the integrity of treatment processes, increases the likelihood for successful reform and promises a reduction in recidivism, and
- treatment when delivered in a targeted manner, can lead to meaningful and lasting reform.

While these assertions appear obvious, contemporary penal practice nonetheless calls for the housing of amenable and nonamenable inmates within the same institutions where contact occurs without restriction. Furthermore, because no effort is currently being undertaken to separate members of these two groups, they attend many of the same treatment programs still in existence. You might be of the initial opinion that this statement contradicts earlier ones concerning the nonamenable inmate's desire to forgo treatment. And while this statement appears contradictory, it is necessary to recognize that nonamenable inmates may attend existing programs out of boredom and even due to staff directive. In fact, compelling inmates to attend treatment programs is a common practice. According to those officials who we interviewed, there are two reasons for compelled attendance. First, it is a management tool for controlling large inmate populations. When inmates are involved in productive pursuits, fewer of them are available to engage in disruptive activities. This practice ensures that during a normal day, the inmate population is reduced to smaller, more manageable groups that spend their limited time and energy on activities that do not threaten institutional operations. Admittedly, this is a self-serving practice intended to benefit the institution. Second, a majority of staff that we interviewed openly acknowledged that they have encouraged inmates to attend programming in spite of their interest or disinterest in treatment. These employees reasoned that this encouragement motivates inmates toward reform. Of course, they believe that when amenable and nonamenable inmates interact within a therapeutic setting, the nonamenable inmate may, through osmosis (for lack of a better word), become amenable. However, this practice may ultimately prove to be counterproductive to treatment for the following reasons:

- the mere presence of the nonamenable inmate within a therapeutic setting may degrade the treatment process (remember your school's class clown and how disruptive his/her presence was to the educational process), and
- by forcing members of these two groups to interact, the nonamenable inmate is more likely to challenge the convictions of the amenable inmate than for the opposite to occur (remember, energy flows from a negative to a positive orientation, suggesting that the direction of influence between nonamenable and amenable inmates is corrupting in nature).

While it is admirable for staff to encourage participation in treatment programs, proponents of specialization assert that nonamenable inmates will challenge the convictions of those who are amenable. After all, nonamenable inmates are, in all probability, more assertive and proficient at manipulating others than are their amenable counterparts. This ensures that they are well positioned to either intentionally or unintentionally impede reform initiatives. Because amenable inmates often lack extensive criminal experience, they may be especially vulnerable for being controlled and exploited by those who are more experienced and invested in criminality. But what do nonamenable inmates gain from this manipulation? Be patient and allow us a few additional comments before we provide the answer. Meanwhile consider the following observation that is borrowed from the *Handbook*:

> Little consideration is given to the kinds of housing and types of persons with which he (the amenable inmate) will associate in his living quarters. His response to the entire program is frequently conditioned by those with whom he lives.

This excerpt suggests an absolute necessity for the separation of these two groups. To permit nonamenable inmates to attend existing treatment programs along with those who are amenable ignores the possibility that a waste of time, energy and resources may occur. Therefore, early advocates of specialization endorsed selectivity in the delivery of treatment based on the premise that nonamenable inmates may monopolize and divert the attention of treatment specialists, ultimately impeding reform efforts. For example, consider the following statement (also taken from the *Handbook*):

> To attempt to give all prisoners all services would be impractical, both because facilities would be diluted to the point where intensive work could not be done with any and second, because such a program would fail to meet the specific needs of individual prisoners.

Thus, the basis for prison specialization rests on the premise that treatment be provided only to amenable inmates in an environment free from the presence of those who either intentionally or unintentionally degrade treatment processes. This is not to suggest that nonamenable inmates be treated more harshly than are amenable inmates. Rather it is simply an acknowledgement that the needs of each group warrant their separation. Consider another observation appearing in the *Handbook*:

> All kinds of individuals are received in prison; experienced, hardened criminals and those who have committed their first offense; the serious escape risk and the person who would leave the institution only by legal process; the adolescent and the aged; the diseased and healthy; the intelligent and the feeble-minded; the insane and psychopathic, and persons who are dangerous to themselves and others. The difficulty in providing a program that will adequately meet the needs and requirements of all these types in one institution is obvious. Efficient segregation is necessary for good custody, discipline, and rehabilitation.

This statement suggests that diversity among inmates is so extensive that it renders the contemporary prison ineffective at meeting their varied needs. Of course, diversity includes demeanor. Advocates of specialization recognize that diversity in demeanor exists, just as there is diversity in age, race and gender. Inmate demeanor must become a necessary consideration during classification processes. The future consequences for failing to do so impact public safety. If the contemporary prison were better able to meet the needs of its inmate population, the crime cycle could be broken and the prison's resources more efficiently applied. The specialized prison is better suited by its very design to meet the needs of each inmate group, ultimately having a greater effect on crime and recidivism rates.

Consider also that the typical inmate socialization process involves the indoctrination of new inmates into the unique subculture of the prison. This process includes the familiarization of new inmates to the typical values, norms and beliefs of those inmates who have established dominance. Since nonamenable inmates are often more assertive and violent, they have successfully established a culture of opposition to correctional intervention. This culture permeates most areas of a prison's operations, especially those that involve inmate and staff interaction as well as those that include, but are not limited to, treatment programs. The existence of this culture became a topic of conversation during our interviews with inmates and staff. Most interviewees commented on having known inmates who desired treatment but were discouraged or otherwise inhibited in this pursuit by their institutional peers. Simply put, nonamenable inmates may be responsible for an overall reduction in the number of inmates who pursue treatment. Certainly, if a culture of opposition exists within the prison, it is being perpetuated by the nonamenable inmate population. But why would nonamenable inmates want to impede existing treatment processes? What could they possibly gain by doing so (returning to our previous question)? In addition to its overall disruptive effect on prison operations, this opposition effectively impedes the ability of officials to detect and investigate the illicit activities of the inmate population, especially its leaders. This leadership derives its power from an underground economy fueled by the acquisition and sale of contraband items, and the provision of prohibited services. As a protective measure, inmates are discouraged from participating in treatment programs since the possibility exists that they might divulge information that could be detrimental to the nonamenable inmate population. Of course, a cooperative relationship between inmates and staff would compromise the ability of the nonamenable inmate population to maintain its control over the prison's culture. By perpetuating a culture of opposition, nonamenable inmates preserve their positions of prominence.

While few suggestions exist about how to implement classification processes that take demeanor into account, it appears implicit that all inmates would, by default, be assumed amenable. In essence, classification specialists would not determine amenability, rather nonamenability. By assuming all inmates to be amenable, the burden of determining otherwise would rest on the shoulders of correctional officials. This would help protect inmate interests by offering each inmate a full range of treatment options. Nothing would be held back since each would, by default, be assumed amenable. But how would nonamenability be determined? Well, inmates are usually quite clear about where they stand on those practices that affect them personally including those pertaining to treatment. Solicited and unsolicited statements would serve to provide insight into each inmate's personality during the normal classification process. Inmates generally either acknowledge or disavow a need for treatment. Thus, a determination of nonamenability might simply begin by asking each inmate how he/she feels about it during initial classification processes. However, since humans are capable of deception, additional sources of information that include staff observations, a review of past criminal involvement and psychological assessments might prove informative. These are the same sources of information that classification officials currently utilize to determine an inmate's security rating. A few indicators of an inmate's nonamenable nature include:

- a vehement refusal to acknowledge criminal actions as personally and socially destructive,
- the development of excuses and/or justifications to minimize or eliminate responsibility, and
- seeing oneself as a victim rather than as an offender.

While additional indicators for nonamenability exist, all reflect an inmate's lack of interest in treatment. Since humans are in a constant state of change and maturation, mechanisms must also be developed to address shifts that may occur in an inmate's demeanor. It is recognized that amenable and nonamenable inmates may, at any given time, have a change of attitude with regard to their desire for treatment. Therefore, an inmate's classification rating cannot be rigid, fixed or final. Instead, provisions must be devised to permit periodic review and reclassification should it become necessary.

Conclusion

In light of slowing prison admissions, an opportunity now exists for penologists to consider proposals that may help reduce recidivism. Early penologists asserted that the prison is fully capable of producing a safer society through offender reform. While contemporary scholarship is replete with evidence suggesting that treatment has lost political support, it is nonetheless the only reasonable solution available to reduce chronic offending.

While attempts at rehabilitation date to the earliest American prisons, its contemporary pursuit was dealt a crippling blow during the 1970s when scholars increasingly proclaimed it unachievable. The anti-reform attack that was launched, coupled with the media's coverage of the riots at Attica (1971) and the Penitentiary of New Mexico (1980), persuaded officials nationwide to reject treatment ideology. Yet in reality investigations into these riots found that they were not fueled by an inmate population that was beyond help but rather by an institutional sterility that embraced administrative mismanagement and inhumane living conditions. Nonetheless, the political machinery withdrew its support for treatment. The control and containment of growing inmate populations became the paramount objective of the prison. Thus, recidivism as a measure of effectiveness was increasingly replaced with the notion that a prison's value could be determined solely by the number of inmates it housed. In the absence of reform ideology, the prison became incrementally harsh and the existence of amenable inmates largely forgotten.

When considering recidivism, one must recognize that incarceration changes inmates either for the better or worse as reflected in recidivism rates. About two thirds of all ex-inmates eventually reoffend, most within 36 months after release. Interestingly enough, this fact is used to justify broadened get-tough sanctions. In essence, advocates of get tough approaches attack treatment based on high recidivism rates yet refuse to acknowledge that it is a lack of appropriate programming that is contributing to criminality. Unfortunately, recidivism rates will likely remain elevated until therapeutic initiatives are again valued. Advocates of specialization argue that high recidivism rates are a direct testimonial to the impracticality of indiscriminately mixing amenable and nonamenable inmates. Closer attention to recidivism rates would help produce a prison system that seeks to reduce the negative effects of incarceration while enhancing its ability to facilitate inmate reform. Ongoing measurements of recidivism would also ensure that prison officials remain accountable to the citizenry with regard to their performance in promoting public safety.

The consideration of alternative ways to house and treat inmates promotes a national dialogue about the purpose and destiny of the prison. By considering the potential benefits of specialization, penologists are taking a necessary first step toward improving public safety. Officials must now determine whether the indiscriminate mixing of inmates within the prison is sound operational practice or whether it may prove beneficial to break with tradition and adopt a newer approach that is creative, innovative and progressive.

In the next chapter, a series of literary equations are presented and applied in order to establish notional relationships between the natural and social realms. This permits us to offer a number of actions that are intended to help improve the efficiency and effectiveness of the contemporary prison. Each of these literary equations has its origin in the natural sciences and each provides insight into the prison, its operations and the inmate population. These equations pertain to cycles, equilibrium, entanglement, energy and its flow, entropy and expansion. It is concluded that it would be beneficial for public officials to be more progressive in their ideological and operational orientations.

HIGHLIGHTS

- While current get tough approaches to crime are popular, questions persist about the extent to which they promote public safety.
- Proponents of specialization recognize that there are generally two groups of inmates; those who are amenable to therapeutic intervention and those who resist such measures.
- Specialization requires the separation of amenable and nonamenable inmates.
- Classification is the process of determining an inmate's security and treatment requirements.
- Traditionally, inmates were classified as being maximum, medium, or minimum security.
- Historically, an inmate's security rating was also accompanied by a treatment plan based on an assessment of his/her needs.
- The prison has long relied upon rote activity, exhibiting hesitancy in developing and implementing innovative practices.
- Most inmates feel that treatment is given little attention by officials of the prison system.
- Early penologists asserted that treatment would become more effective if delivered within specialized prisons. This would, in turn, reduce the personal, social and financial costs associated with repeated criminality.
- Prison specialization dates to the thirteenth century when officials in England began to separate less serious and less experienced offenders from those displaying a more chronic and hardened demeanor.
- Nonamenable inmates may attend existing treatment programs out of boredom or because of compelled participation.
- Compelled participation in treatment programs is occasionally used to manage large inmate populations and is often believed to motivate nonamenable inmates toward reform.

- Nonamenable inmates are often more assertive and proficient at manipulation than are their amenable counterparts.

- Early advocates of specialization endorsed selectivity in the delivery of treatment based on the premise that nonamenable inmates may monopolize the attention of treatment specialists.

- It is impractical for one institution to attempt to give all prisoners all services.

- Inmate diversity is so extensive that it renders the contemporary prison incapable of meeting this population's needs. Diversity not only includes age, race and gender, but also demeanor.

- By failing to meet the needs of its inmate population, the prison is perpetuating the crime cycle and unnecessarily taxing the resources of the criminal justice system.

- Since nonamenable inmates are often more assertive and violent than are amenable ones, they have successfully established a culture of opposition to correctional intervention.

- A culture of opposition serves to disrupt prison operations and effectively impedes the ability of officials to detect and investigate the illicit activities of the inmate population.

- By perpetuating a culture of opposition, nonamenable inmate leaders preserve their positions of prominence.

- It appears implicit that all inmates, by default, should initially be assumed amenable. In essence, classification specialists would not determine amenability, rather nonamenability.

- Determinations of nonamenability might begin by asking each inmate how he/she feels about treatment during initial classification processes. These statements would then be considered along with additional sources of information including staff observations, a review of past criminal involvement and psychological assessments.

- Since humans are in a constant state of change, mechanisms must be developed to address shifts that may occur in an inmate's demeanor. It is recognized that amenable and nonamenable inmates may, at any given time, have a change of attitude with regard to their desire for treatment.

- The media's coverage of the Attica and the Penitentiary of New Mexico riots led to diminished support for reform initiatives.

- One must recognize that incarceration usually changes inmates for the worse.

- Advocates of specialization argue that high recidivism rates are the result of the indiscriminate mixing of amenable and nonamenable inmates.

- Closer attention to recidivism rates would produce a prison system that seeks to reduce the negative effects of incarceration while enhancing its ability to facilitate inmate reform.

QUESTIONS

1). Does the prison rely more heavily upon rote activity than innovative practice? Explain. Does the prison exhibit timelessness in its physical and operational characteristics? Explain.

2). What attitudes and actions of the inmate population perpetuate criminality? What attitudes and actions of staff perpetuate criminality? Be as specific as possible.

3). How valid is the observation that any contemporary proposal calling for the establishment of specialized prisons must be historically based in order to be perceived as legitimate? Explain.

4). Does tradition have a paralyzing effect upon the prison? Why or why not?

5). Should inmate demeanor be considered during classification procedures? How is demeanor similar to or different from other characteristics including sex, age and criminal history?

6). Is there a difference between separating inmates for disciplinary purposes and separating them for preventative purposes? Explain.

7). How might amenable inmates be discreetly and/or overtly discouraged from participating in treatment? Is it reasonable to assume that even if nonamenable inmates do not engage in disruptive actions or openly defy authority that they may nonetheless display subtle attitudes or behaviors that might discourage others from participating in therapeutic initiatives? Explain.

8). What is meant by the phrase "culture of opposition" when describing the contemporary prison environment? Who has created this culture and what benefits does it provide, if any, to the inmate population?

9). What are the advantages and disadvantages to assuming amenability during initial classification processes? Explain. Compare this approach to one that assumes nonamenability.

CHAPTER NINE
Literary Equations

The question "WHAT IF...?" has great power. It allows us to see into the future, anticipate problems and create workable solutions.

In the previous chapters we used the natural sciences to examine the contemporary prison. By applying biological and physical principles to the social realm, a greater understanding of the prison is achieved. And while we are in no way suggesting that anything but free will controls the actions of humans or institutions, social scientists could benefit from considering that which is already known about the natural realm. If nothing else, nature quickly reveals our vulnerability to uncertainty. It is also through a consideration of natural processes that we may better understand our behaviors, relationships and collective responsibility to provide for our common welfare. While our quest to understand ourselves and our place in the universe is in its infancy, we are confident that humankind is capable of understanding anything we set our minds to - the only obstacle being our hesitancy to fully apply our cognitive powers. Our ability to obtain a greater understanding of our natural and social environments allows us to improve our circumstances. We must embrace this responsibility and use those tools that will advance our understanding of ourselves as social beings.

This chapter has admittedly proven much more difficult to compose than any of the previous chapters. Why you might ask? Well, within each of the previous chapters the task was relatively simple. All that was required was to take a principle or theory from the natural sciences and apply it to the social realm. Doing so presented little difficulty. The present chapter on the other hand requires that the cumulative content of the previous chapters and their assertions be integrated in such a way that a "eureka" moment is achieved. Of course, "eureka" is an exclamation that is made when a breakthrough in thought or understanding occurs. Such a breakthrough within the context of the present work requires a degree of innovative and creative wrangling that exceeds that which is normally required in academic writing.

While contemplating an appropriate manner in which to pursue a eureka moment, we decided to re-read previous chapters to see if an approach might magically reveal itself. In doing so we became intrigued by four words that seemed to materialize from nowhere. As we began to seriously consider the appropriateness of using these four words as the basis for this chapter, we became convinced that these words would allow us to draw a number of conclusions to showcase the ability of the natural sciences to provide insight into the social realm. These words are, "if…and…then…otherwise". While there is nothing magical about these words either singularly or collectively, the sequence in which they are arranged does permit a determination to be made about those relationships that may exist between the natural and social realms as well as between their respective concepts and theories. More specifically, this 4-word sequence allows us to visualize real and hypothetical relationships, apply these relationships to other realms, determine consequences realistically arising from these relationships and then determine an appropriate course of action to address unwanted outcomes. We also refer to this sequence as a literary equation since it serves a function similar to that which is served by a mathematical calculation.

In the pages that follow we provide a series of statements that will establish notional relationships between the natural and social realms. This allows us to offer a number of actions that may, if implemented, increase the efficacy of the prison. The material appearing within this chapter is provided simply for its theoretical and conceptual value and in no way suggests that we are controlled by anything other than free will. However, we continue to assert that a consideration of the natural world provides us with a greater understanding of ourselves and our actions. Such an acknowledgement allows us to act more intelligently, potentially maximizing the efficiency and effectiveness of our social institutions.

Before presenting these literary equations it is important to remember that this book contains a number of themes. These themes, when considered collectively, reveal the seamlessness of their relationship to one another and their relevance to our present efforts. These themes are as follows:

- natural events tend to be cyclical,
- it is difficult for natural systems to maintain equilibrium and balance,
- entanglement occurs within the natural realm,
- energy always seeks it lowest level and flows from a negative toward a positive state,
- entropy increases over time, and
- expansion leads to a dissipation of energy whereas contraction has a re-energizing effect.

It now becomes necessary to develop a number of assertions that link natural and social phenomena. This will allow a comparison to be made between realms that culminate in a "To Do" list intended to enhance the prison's ability to break the crime cycle.

Literary Equations at Work

The first theme contained within this book is that natural events tend to be cyclical. Consider the seasons, the ebb and flow of the ocean's tides and even lunar phases as evidence proving this assertion. Now let's apply this theme to the social realm:

IF natural events are cyclical,

AND if the natural and social realms are comparable,

THEN those penal practices that have lost favor will, in time, enjoy renewed support.

OTHERWISE innovative and progressive correctional practices have little social value and once abandoned will forever be lost, ensuring that the prison's actions are increasingly based on convenience rather than their ability to promote public safety.

Remember the hypothetical pendulum mentioned previously? It was used to suggest that cycles or rhythms are found in the social realm. Based upon this probability, one can predict a future resurgence in treatment ideologies and practices. It would appear prudent then to prepare a group of treatment-minded professionals to assume leadership positions within the prison in preparation for this event. Conversely, it would appear equally prudent for correctional institutions to cease their current practice of systematically erasing all references to treatment and rehabilitation from their mission statements. Those treatment programs that are currently operational should be permitted to continue without further hindrance. Any approach that minimizes the importance of treatment or degrades rehabilitation while ignoring the cyclical nature of correctional intervention is short sighted and reactionary in nature. In essence, we should recognize the cyclical character of social and institutional behaviors and act to ensure that prison staff, institutional mission statements and correctional programs are grounded in an ideology that provides a lasting benefit to society regardless of the ebb and flow of the political du jour.

As we have already determined, it is difficult for natural systems to maintain homeostasis. When equilibrium is not maintained, a system begins to suffer and loses its ability to function in an efficient and effective manner. If the system is biological in nature, it may enter a period of decline and eventually become terminal. Systems of a non-biological nature act in a similar fashion. For example, if a social system is not able to use energy efficiently, it too may enter a period of decline and could ultimately cease to exist:

> IF natural systems experience difficulty in maintaining equilibrium,
>
> AND if the natural and social realms are comparable,
>
> THEN it is imperative that a balance be achieved between an organization's objectives and its actions.
>
> OTHERWISE a state of confusion, homeostatic imbalance and conflict results which impedes an organization's ability to maximize its benefit to society.

There must always be a balance between an organization's objectives and its actions. Even though efforts have been made to distance itself from rehabilitation, the prison is still viewed by most citizens as the component of the criminal justice system that is responsible for breaking the crime cycle. Citizens also recognize the current imbalance between the prison's traditional objectives and its actions. This imbalance communicates an inconsistent message to the citizenry and the inmate population. For example, what message do inmates receive from a system that describes itself as being "correctional" in nature yet refuses to acknowledge the value of education, vocational training or therapeutic pursuits? Such an inconsistency suggests that the system is more interested in management than in helping inmates improve their circumstances.

When pondering the prison's ability to promote pro-social behaviors and improve the circumstances of its inmates, we must consider entanglement. In doing so, the value in establishing positive personal relationships as a mechanism to break the crime cycle becomes evident. Positive relationships are instrumental in providing offenders with the support, coaching and mentorship necessary for rehabilitation. Positive relationships encourage positive behaviors whereas negative relationships encourage negative behavior through the establishment and solidification of destructive attitudes, thought-processes and actions. By creating an environment where constructive associations are encouraged, entanglement can be used to reduce chronic offending and lower recidivism rates. Consider the following:

> IF particles become entangled,
>
> AND if the natural and social realms are comparable,
>
> THEN manipulation of similar social processes could prove effective at helping break the crime cycle.
>
> OTHERWISE the prison serves as little more than a conduit through which anti-social attitudes and behaviors become more affixed and criminality more engrained.

The relationship described above clearly acknowledges the power of positive peer associations, environmental manipulation, inmate classification and the need for institutional operations to promote pro-social attitudes and behaviors. The relationship between peer influence and behavior cannot be disputed! There have been multiple national initiatives that warn our nation's youth about the effects of negative peer pressure. Yet few professionals recognize that this process also works in reverse and can be harnessed for our collective benefit. If we promote positive peer associations within our prisons, offenders and society might both benefit. In essence, were we to reverse current processes, capitalizing on positive peer associations while minimizing negativity, we could improve our ability to break the crime cycle.

Having addressed entanglement, we can now consider energy and its propensity to seek its lowest level and to flow from a negative toward a positive state. For example:

> IF energy always flows from a state of excitement toward a state of rest,
>
> AND if the natural and social realms are comparable,
>
> THEN it becomes imperative for officials to support treatment.

OTHERWISE energy will decline to the point where treatment either ceases to exist or exists simply for its ability to portray the prison as a humanitarian institution.

FURTHERMORE

IF energy flows from a negative toward a positive state,

AND if the natural and social realms are comparable,

THEN efforts must be undertaken to ensure that negatively oriented inmates are rendered incapable of corrupting those displaying a more amenable disposition.

OTHERWISE the prison will continue to prove ineffective at breaking the crime cycle.

Of course, each of these assertions easily lends itself to methods designed specifically to divert, manage and utilize energy in all of its various forms. If you recall, the social equivalents to physical energy were identified as interest, effort, time, resources and peer influence. Each of these energies, in numerous ways and to varying degrees, contains the ability to motivate, mobilize and invigorate people and institutions toward the accomplishment of socially productive endeavors. The key to achieving most goals, it would appear, is to understand the nature of energy and how to apply it in an efficient and effective manner, and nowhere is this more essential than in corrections.

Furthermore, as we have already seen, systems tend to gravitate toward entropy. An entropic state is said to afflict a system when it functions improperly or performs at less than an optimal level. Stated a bit differently, both natural and social systems tend to degrade over time, becoming less efficient and less effective at accomplishing their objectives:

IF natural systems tend to move toward an entropic state,

AND if the natural and social realms are comparable,

THEN it becomes necessary for officials to recognize those objectives that are socially beneficial, pursue them vigorously and to measure their achievement.

OTHERWISE officials will increasingly downplay the importance of labor-intensive activities, will identify and pursue objectives that require lower energy and fiscal outlays, and will dismiss the importance of all performance measures that do not reflect positively upon their actions.

Recently, the American Correctional Association has openly questioned the value of measuring recidivism as a way to gauge the prison's ability to safeguard the public's interest. It has taken such a position in an effort to distance itself from the obvious failure of the modern prison to achieve its fullest potential. There is an effort within corrections to identify and use performance measures that are more easily controlled and achieved. These measures include, among others, the number of days that an institution has gone without experiencing an assault, the number of contraband items discovered during routine shake-downs, even the number of disciplinary actions undertaken each month. And while these measures provide insight into how a prison operates, the only measure that really matters to the average citizen is recidivism. After all, it is the only measure that directly relates to the public's long-term safety.

Finally, it has been observed that expansion leads to a loss of energy whereas contraction produces an abundance of energy. This observation allows us to discern a great deal about natural and social processes. Consider the following:

IF expansion eventually results in decline,

AND if the natural and social realms are comparable,

THEN it is imperative that authorities acknowledge that continued expansion will result in reduced energy levels and a growing reliance on passive behaviors as a means to conserve scarce resources.

OTHERWISE if left uncontrolled, expansion will produce a system that is increasingly cold, detached and impersonal, all of which impede the

> prison's ability to break the crime cycle. Contraction, were it to occur, would reverse this trend, increase energy levels and facilitate proactive intervention.

This observation suggests that when a social system is placed under stress whereby great demands are made upon its finite energy, labor and fiscal levels, choices must be made about resource allocation and program reduction and/or elimination. Decisions of this kind have a direct impact on an institution's objectives and its actions. In the case of the prison, expansion has produced huge inmate populations that consume large amounts of resources. In response, prison authorities have cut most non-essential programs in an attempt to meet the immediate needs of their inmates. The risk assumed when engaging in this process is that over time, the prison will become a passive institution that either downplays or altogether forgets the value of treatment, with traditional performance measures suffering a similar fate.

"To Do" List

Having applied these literary equations to the six themes previously identified, the next order of business is to determine what actions must be undertaken to improve the modern prison. We must determine how to apply what we know, or think we know, about the similarities existing between the natural and social realms in order to repair and prevent future problems. The material to follow can't possibly address all the problems plaguing the prison. To do so would require the writing of many books and a substantial investment of resources. Instead, we will restrict our comments to those observations appearing previously in this chapter. We will also provide a logical course of action that, if followed, might minimize or remediate the effects of current practices. And finally, the reader should understand that while there are numerous methods that can be brought to bear on a problem, an ounce or two of creative, progressive and innovative thought might yield a plethora of solutions that prove effective.

When considering our first literary equation pertaining to the cyclical nature of the social realm, it becomes apparent that treatment may soon gain prominence and re-emerge as a correctional pursuit. As we predicted earlier, this movement will, in all probability, begin in the near future. As suggested, there are a number of actions that we should adopt in preparation for this event. These actions will help ensure that treatment is given every opportunity to achieve a high level of effectiveness. Among these actions are the following:

- the development of a new crop of correctional practitioners thoroughly educated in treatment theory and practice. These individuals should be familiar with the prison's history, the prison's traditional objectives, methods to create networks to complement therapeutic endeavors, and the latest advances in educational, vocational and therapeutic techniques that are supported by performance-based evidence,
- the willingness of practitioners to modify programs to more precisely meet the varying needs of inmate populations, recognizing a diversity of challenges that may be region, crime, age, and gender specific,
- an effort to increase familiarity of staff with those programs being offered within their own institutions. The best way to implement this action is through intensive instruction given during new employee training sessions. There must also be a similar effort targeting regular employees during in-service training. This will ensure that all employees are provided consistent information and are familiar with their institution's programs as well as their role in the treatment process,
- the cessation of all efforts to erase references to treatment and rehabilitation from departmental mission statements and related guiding documents. Those references that have been removed should be restored. This will help ensure that an institution's ideological underpinnings are consistent with social expectations pertaining to its operations,
- an effort to support those treatment programs that are still in existence. These programs should be protected from further financial pirating. Once protected, they should be subjected to critical review with improvements being implemented as needed, and

- the measurement of recidivism rates so that trends can be identified and the effectiveness of treatment initiatives determined. Recidivism must be recognized as the single most important measure of the prison's ability to promote public safety, and as such, rehabilitation must be given top priority.

If the prison's ideological and operational orientations are cyclical in nature, then we must act accordingly. All attempts to erase rehabilitation from the prison's traditional objectives will, in essence, result in a state of imbalance. Furthermore, the ebb and flow of rehabilitation's popularity may be controlled if careful measurements are taken with regard to recidivism. Provided that the effectiveness of treatment can be statistically established, future attempts to reduce therapeutic programs would prove difficult. This would help ensure a lasting ideological balance that hasn't existed in over three decades.

When speaking of balance, it has been observed that all systems experience difficulty in maintaining equilibrium. If such an observation is accurate and if the prison like other systems is in a constant struggle to balance its ideologies, objectives and actions, then a number of suggestions appear appropriate to help restore and maintain consistency in operations. These suggestions include a need for correctional officials to:

- acknowledge that rehabilitation was the primary objective of the prison for most of its history,
- introduce all staff to the prison's history with an emphasis being placed on an understanding of its traditional operational objectives and their interconnectedness,
- acknowledge that corrections is an active process that requires an investment from all parties involved, and
- acknowledge that the present warehousing approach, based on incarceration without treatment, is passive in nature and as such fails to produce any incentive for personal improvement.

In essence, balance requires familiarity with the prison's history and an acknowledgement that any attempt to distance itself from treatment will result in an approach that places the prison in conflict with its prescribed purpose. When an imbalance occurs, it produces a state of confusion and operational uncertainty whereby all institutional actions are reduced to their most basic denominator, and in the case of the prison, this has resulted in the warehousing of offenders with little or no concern for how this approach impacts public safety. Balance requires a concern for the future, and while incapacitation has an immediate social benefit, treatment produces both immediate as well as future benefits.

Contemporary correctional officials appear to have forgotten the importance of relationships. As we have already noted, parents have long warned their children to avoid those individuals perceived to be a bad influence. This observation suggests that we are shaped by our associations. For example, if one wishes to acquire the characteristics of a genius then one should associate with those who possess that quality. Similarly, if one is surrounded by those exhibiting anti-social attitudes, the chances that he/she will become anti-social increase. Positive relationships are so significant to rehabilitation that they may be among the most important factors necessary when seeking to break the crime cycle. The flipside of this observation is that negative associations are one of the greatest contributors to criminality. As such, correctional officials must:

- acknowledge the importance of relationships, realizing that positive associations lead to positive behaviors whereas negative associations lead to negative behaviors,
- seek to create an environment that minimizes negativity by building positive relationships between staff and inmates,
- create mentoring programs that extend beyond the prison's walls to allow discharged or paroled offenders to obtain advice and guidance from prison staff and peer mentors, and
- understand that the contemporary inmate culture has been created and is perpetuated by those who are criminally experienced, predatory in nature and by those who seek to maintain their positions of prominence. By allowing such a culture to exist,

> amenable inmates have little choice but to adopt the characteristics of those inmates in power. Until this flow of negative energy ceases, there is little hope that there will be an improvement in recidivism rates.

The culture of the prison has decayed to such an extent that little or no attempt is made to disguise inmate efforts to promote chaos, discord and further criminality. We have witnessed inmates hold classes in plain view, and with full knowledge of a prison's administration, on the latest techniques to manufacture illegal drugs, steal cars, and to incapacitate law enforcement officers. Inmates have become brazen about their actions. In a culture shaped and controlled by hardened and violent offenders, amenable inmates stand little chance. In essence, resistance by the amenable inmate is futile! Those treatment programs that are still in existence are rendered ineffective since few inmates, if any, attend. Empty prison classrooms are normal since attendance is considered a punishable transgression by inmate leadership. A negative culture that promotes negative relationships proves counterproductive to the interest of the prison and society. Why this culture has been allowed to persist remains one of the great mysteries of contemporary corrections.

As we have witnessed within the natural realm, energy always seeks its lowest level and flows from a negative toward a positive state. If physical and social energies behave similarly, then energy levels within our correctional institutions will continue to decrease, ultimately robbing prison officials of their desire and ability to rehabilitate offenders. In other words, officials become progressively lazy over time. For example, most fields have experienced a golden era characterized by high energy levels, output and advances in understanding. These eras are typically followed by decreased energy and productivity levels when fewer breakthroughs occur. We can liken this to normal maturation processes whereby youth is characterized by energy, exuberance, exploration and discovery. Old age, however, is viewed as a period of low energy, low activity and decline. Institutions follow a trajectory similar to that of all living things, and unless intervention occurs, are doomed to a similar fate. Toward this end, when energy is scarce, an institution will seek to adopt those ideologies, objectives, practices and performance measures that justify decreased effort. When this occurs, it is a sure sign that the officials of an institution have resigned themselves to fate.

We have also seen that energy flows from a negative toward a positive state. If we are to create a mental image of this event, we might imagine two inmates, one with a negative orientation and the other with a positive orientation. When these inmates interact, an interesting process commences. The nonamenable inmate who is typically more assertive and violent becomes dominant. As such, he/she exerts influence over the actions of the other. Negatively oriented inmates tend to oppose correctional intervention and stand in stark contrast to positively oriented inmates who, by their very nature, are more amenable toward treatment. Placed into a culture created by violent inmates and controlled by those who oppose treatment, amenable inmates find themselves unable to resist this influence or withstand its effects. After all, the prison's culture is characterized by an inescapable negativity making it difficult to resist assimilation. Thus, energy in this situation flows from the negative end of the continuum toward the positive, suggesting that a negatively oriented inmate will exert influence over those of a positive orientation. Given time, the positively oriented inmate has little choice but to adopt a negative disposition. Assuming this to be the case, a number of actions should be undertaken. These include:

- an acknowledgement that prison personnel have become complacent in protecting the amenable inmate from the corrupting influence of those with a negative orientation, and in doing, they have similarly failed to act in the best interest of society. Prison personnel are now less willing to engage the inmate population in socially beneficial activities than at any previous time in history,
- the identification, recruitment, employment and retention of professionally oriented and highly motivated individuals to fill correctional vacancies. This is vitally important since prison

employees are notoriously transient in nature. If effectiveness is being sought, then a professional orientation becomes a necessity,

- similarly, an infusion of needed resources must occur. The prison's programs must be given the resources needed to ensure that they effectively engage the inmate population in educational, vocational and therapeutic pursuits. There must be a sufficient number of these programs, all of which are of the highest possible quality,
- there must be an acknowledgement that the inmate culture is capable of nullifying attempts at treatment. In fact, inmates have appropriated the power to shape the very nature of the prison itself, creating an environment that is counterproductive to rehabilitation, and
- classification processes must determine an inmate's level of amenability. Based upon this determination, appropriate actions can be undertaken to protect those inmates who have a positive orientation from those displaying a more defiant and predatory disposition.

We remain convinced, as we have now for two decades, that if the average citizen were to visit a prison, he/she would be appalled at the level of idleness among the inmate population. On any typical day, inmates can be found sunbathing, watching daytime television programs, loitering about the prison yard, and playing handball, basketball and baseball. While these activities are admittedly harmless in nature, they do little to break the crime cycle or to prepare inmates for release. Compounding this problem is the fact that since inmates are not being engaged in any meaningful manner, their skills, be they cognitive or employment related, tend to deteriorate. When one doesn't use his/her skills, those skills are often lost! Add to this mix a negatively charged environment where violence and predation are valued and even celebrated, and you have a recipe for failure. There is a pervasive belief that the prison, as a manifestation of the government, has society's best interests at heart and acts accordingly. Such a belief is misplaced. Efforts must be undertaken to increase the level of positive energy in our prisons and to simultaneously break the process whereby negativity is allowed to dominate.

Similarly, the prison's level of entropy is increasing. As you may recall, entropy can be thought of as the inability of a system to effectively utilize energy. The use of energy within a social system is often hindered by an internal confusion about the goals or objectives of the system itself. In the prison, entropy may be thought of as a pervasive confusion among staff about their role in the correctional process. In other words, there are competing and conflicting messages. We have already noted that rehabilitation is no longer an official objective of the prison, yet a majority of all staff (and citizens, alike) recognize a value in treatment and expect the prison to act accordingly. When a disjunction between expectations and actions exist, a situation is created whereby progressively fewer staff may recognize or care about their ability to promote societal interests. In fact, as bureaucrats, prison officials have little incentive to care about the interests of society. As an isolated institution that is largely hidden from public view, officials are able to operate with little or no oversight. Instead, their focus tends to be on those challenges of a more internal and immediate nature. These challenges have become the prison's most important operational determinants with little thought being given for the long-term effects of any specific action or inaction. Such an orientation results in an inability of the prison to effectively accomplish any but its most basic objective which is the housing of its inmate population. If entropy is measured by a loss of effectiveness in providing for the public's long-term safety (as revealed through measures of recidivism), then there is little doubt that the level of disorder within our prisons has exponentially increased over the past three decades. To reverse this trend, officials must:

- clearly publish the mission of the prison. This will ensure that all respective parties are familiar with its overall purpose as well as their role in helping it achieve its stated objectives. The achievement of these objectives should be evaluated at least annually. If they are not achieved, then corrective action should be taken. For the prison, this action may result in a change in administration; for the employee, it may result in remedial training;

and for the inmate, it may result in a loss of good time credit or a modification to his/her daily routine,

- establish harmony between social expectations and the mission of the prison itself. When achieved, a more unified and consistent operational approach will result. A citizen review committee serving in an oversight and advisory capacity would help ensure that the prison's actions are consistent with its mission, that its actions are transparent in nature, and that the prison is held accountable by its constituency, and
- stop pirating resources from so called nonessential programs and services and instead reduce costs through better management practices. At some point pirating creates an environment where the prison becomes an active participant in the perpetuation of the crime cycle rather than a mechanism by which it is broken.

Furthermore, entropy is not a terribly difficult process to prevent, especially within the social realm. Its reversal and prevention only requires that the operational objectives and actions of the prison are consistent with public expectations. In other words, convenience should never be the operational standard by which our prisons function - rather, prison officials should always seek to advance societal interests by aggressively promoting treatment and rehabilitation. If prison officials refuse to gauge their performance by any other measure than recidivism, then accountability is little more than an illusion. Currently, the prison is evading accountability by operating without constituency oversight. Such an approach has directly contributed to both the continuing failure and subsequent expansion of the modern prison.

And finally, we must consider expansion. No single event in history has had a greater impact on the prison's operations or ideological orientation than its recent growth. We must remember that the prison is never closed nor is it permitted to post a "no vacancy" sign. To some extent we remain sympathetic with the prison's inability to control its growth. In essence, the prison's growth is largely determined by the police and judiciary. We also understand the reasons that have prompted prison administrators to pirate resources from treatment programs. We know firsthand that when confronted with an insatiable demand for its services, stressed institutions will seek to restructure themselves as a self-protective measure. In the case of the prison, officials reduced its objectives to just one; simple confinement, a passive approach that minimizes expenditures. However, our understanding does little to mitigate the fact that prison administrators have had more than three decades now to regain their wits. There has been ample time for cooler minds to prevail. And yet, officials appear to have found a sense of purpose and even professional permanency in the prison's expansion. Few officials appear to understand our contention that the prison must measure its effectiveness not by expansion but by contraction. A decrease in its size and a diminishing need for its services (i.e. reduced recidivism) should be the prison's only measure of effectiveness. In essence, the prison should work tirelessly to put itself out of business. Were officials to concede this point, they would have little choice but to act accordingly. Toward this end, governmental officials must recognize that:

- the recent expansion of the prison has forced it into a state of paralysis whereby staff and inmates alike are unclear about its guiding ideology, its overall mission and even its operational objectives. This has, in turn, left members of both groups unsure of their role in the correctional process,
- expansion has produced an inmate culture that is not treatment friendly but rather, seeks to legitimize and promote continued criminality,
- expansion has produced a cold, clinical, and detached approach to staff-inmate interactions. This has done little to facilitate reform among inmates and has instead helped produce a level of animosity that fuels anti-social, anti-establishment attitudes,
- expansion has resulted in an operational approach that is unbalanced, ignoring the long-term interests of society,
- contraction, on the other hand, could help restore previous energy levels, making the prison a more active and engaged institution, and
- contraction would free up resources that might, in turn, be re-tasked to promote treatment, rehabilitation and public safety.

The most significant problem facing the modern prison administrator is determining how to effectively manage a massive inmate population that has an insatiable hunger for scarce resources. All available resources have been re-routed to ensure that the most basic needs of this population are being met. However, if this population were to decrease in size, a redistribution of resources would help promote a treatment orientation. Currently, few resources are being used for treatment. This frequently prompts inmates to indict the prison for its lack of interest in rehabilitation. Such an observation speaks volumes. Expansion has always been associated with decline and eventual death. Contraction, on the other hand, has always been associated with an abundance of energy and resources. Energy and resources are essential to the accomplishment of all tasks. If energy and resources are scarce, only the minimum is achieved. If energy and resources are abundant and properly applied, anything becomes possible.

Conclusion

It is difficult to select material to present in a chapter's conclusion. To do so an author must consider all pertinent information in order to determine its significance and applicability. As such, a few observations seem especially appropriate. First, it is essential for correctional ideologies and practices to move beyond current short-term approaches that do little to advance the causes of penology. A shortsighted orientation works to the detriment of the offender and society by ensuring that only those challenges that require immediate attention are pursued while all other challenges, especially those pertaining to the future behaviors of offenders, receive little if any consideration. Therefore, it would appear necessary for correctional professionals to think in generational terms. By forcing prison officials to be forward thinking in their ideological orientation, they would be compelled to acknowledge the value of treatment and the importance of measuring recidivism rates. Simply put, a generational approach promotes proactive efforts and strict accountability.

We must also ensure that the actions of our correctional practitioners are consistent with this generational ideology. Without a balance between ideology and action, all efforts will be doomed to failure. Balance requires harmony and interconnectedness between thought and practice. In its absence, correctional efforts, in whatever form they take, will be unable to break the criminogenic cycle. The present confusion that permeates correctional thoughts and practices has relegated the prison to being little more than a human warehouse. For an institution founded on hope and redemption, a failure of this nature is a condemnation of humanity. Correctional efforts must acknowledge the value of humanity and provide as many benefits to the next generation as possible.

We must also recognize that citizens are the prison's constituency. As a public institution, the prison exists for our benefit and is of course, taxpayer supported. Therefore, the public should become more engaged in its operations. To this end, there must be efforts by citizen groups as well as prison officials to facilitate this participation. Since the prison has historically been an isolated and secluded institution, it has operated in a closed manner free from the normal restraints associated with citizen oversight. Input from an institution's constituency on expectations and performance measures would increase accountability. Citizen advisory boards have proven valuable in the law enforcement community. Having similar advisory boards within our institutions would promote social awareness, accountability, and might ensure that officials become serious about breaking the crime cycle. Since these institutions are publicly funded, citizens must assume a more active role in their management.

Similarly, the only meaningful way to assess the prison's ability to act in a socially productive manner is through a consideration of recidivism. No other measure so directly or so succinctly reflects the ability or inability of the prison to promote public safety. We should hold our officials accountable for their continuing failures. Without direct intervention and strict accountability, recidivism will not decrease. It is clear that action is needed.

It also appears especially appropriate to suggest that we begin making greater use of literary equations. These word sequences permit us to visualize both real and hypothetical relationships, apply these relationships to our particular areas of interest, determine consequences arising from these relationships, and then determine an appropriate course of action to address unwanted outcomes. This sequencing, combined with a good dose of innovative, creative and progressive thinking, allows us to formulate possible solutions to the many problems confronting the contemporary prison.

Finally, we feel as if the eureka moment that we were attempting to achieve within this chapter has proven elusive. Perhaps, this is to be expected. After all, this elusiveness reflects the sheer magnitude of the current correctional dilemma. No single observation or statement can comprehensively convey the atrocious conditions of the contemporary prison or the need to address them. Remember, every problem should be viewed as an opportunity for improvement and the contemporary prison presents a great number of opportunities for us to become involved in this process. Perhaps it is this realization that will serve, to whatever extent possible, as the overall theme of this chapter. Eureka! In the next chapter, a few concluding observations are offered. These observations are then followed by a number of predictions pertaining to the future prison.

HIGHLIGHTS

- Nature quickly reminds us of just how vulnerable we are to uncertainties.
- It is through a consideration of natural processes that we may better understand our behaviors, relationships and collective responsibility to provide for our common welfare.
- We are capable of understanding anything we set our minds to, the only obstacle is our hesitancy to fully apply our cognitive powers.
- The words “if, and, then, otherwise” allow us to visualize real and hypothetical relationships, apply these relationships to other realms, determine consequences realistically arising from these relationships, and then determine an appropriate course of action to address unwanted outcomes.
- Cycles or rhythms are found in the social realm. Based upon this observation, one can predict a future resurgence in treatment ideologies and practices.
- Any practice or approach that minimizes the value of rehabilitation is short sighted and reactionary in nature.
- Citizens recognize an imbalance existing between the traditional objectives of the prison and its contemporary actions.
- A balance between an organization’s objectives and its actions should be maintained.
- Even though efforts have been made to distance itself from rehabilitation, the prison is still viewed by most citizens as the component of the justice system that is most responsible for breaking the crime cycle.
- The value in establishing positive personal relationships as a mechanism to break the crime cycle is evident.
- Positive relationships help provide offenders with support, coaching, and mentorship, all of which promote conventional behavior.

- Positive relationships encourage positive behaviors while negative relationships encourage the establishment and solidification of destructive attitudes, thought processes and actions.

- If we were to promote positive peer associations within our prisons, offenders and society would each benefit. In essence, were we to reverse current processes, capitalizing on positive peer associations while minimizing negativity, we would be better positioned to break the crime cycle.

- The key to achieving most goals is to understand the nature of energy and how to apply it in an efficient and effective manner, and nowhere is this needed more than in corrections.

- Recently, the American Correctional Association has openly questioned the value of recidivism as a measure of the prison's ability to safeguard the public's interest.

- A correctional effort exists to identify and use performance measures that are more easily controlled and achieved than are reductions in recidivism rates.

- When confronted with an insatiable demand for services, institutions will seek to restructure themselves as a self-protective measure. In the case of the prison, officials reduced its objectives to just one; simple confinement, a passive approach that minimizes expenditures.

- We must determine how to apply what we know (or think we know) about the similarities between the natural and social realms in order to improve the human condition.

- While there are numerous methods that can be brought to bear on a problem, an ounce or two of creative, progressive and innovative thought might yield a plethora of solutions that prove effective.

- Fluctuations in rehabilitation's popularity can be controlled if the effectiveness of treatment programs is conclusively established. This would help provide a balance that hasn't existed in over three decades.

- Operational balance requires familiarity with the prison's history and an acknowledgement that any attempt to distance itself from treatment will result in an orientation that places the prison in conflict with its prescribed purpose.

- A correctional environment steeped in treatment will, by its very nature, encourage inmates to develop and maintain positive peer associations.
- Many correctional officials have forgotten the importance of relationships.
- Positive relationships are essential when seeking to break the crime cycle.
- The culture of the prison has decayed to such an extent that little or no attempt is made to disguise organized inmate efforts to promote chaos, discord and further criminality.
- If physical and social energies behave similarly, then energy levels within our correctional institutions will, if left unaddressed, continue to decrease, completely robbing our prisons of their ability to rehabilitate offenders.
- Institutions follow a trajectory similar to that of all living things, and unless intervention occurs, are doomed to a similar fate. Toward this end, when energy is scarce, an institution will seek to adopt those ideologies, objectives, practices and performance measures that justify a decreased effort. When this occurs, it is a sure sign that officials have resigned the prison to fate.
- Placed into a culture created by violent inmates and controlled by those who oppose treatment, the amenable inmate finds him/herself unable to resist negative influences or withstand their effects.
- If the average citizen were to visit a prison, he/she would be appalled at the level of idleness among the inmate population.
- Since inmates are not being engaged in any meaningful manner, their skills, whether cognitive or employment related, tend to deteriorate. When one doesn't use his/her skills, those skills are often lost!
- There is a belief that the prison as a manifestation of the government has the public's best interests at heart and acts accordingly. Such a belief is misplaced.
- Efforts must be taken to increase the level of positive energy in our prisons and to simultaneously break the process whereby negativity is allowed to dominate.

- The efficient and effective use of energy within a social system is often hindered by an internal confusion about the goals or objectives of the system itself.

- When a disjunction between expectations and actions occur, a situation is created whereby progressively fewer staff may recognize or care about their ability to promote societal interests.

- As bureaucrats, prison officials have little to no incentive to care about the interests of society.

- As an isolated institution that is largely hidden from public view, prisons are able to operate with little or no oversight.

- If entropy is measured by increased recidivism, then there is little doubt that disorder within the prison has exponentially increased over the past three decades.

- Entropy is not difficult to prevent, especially within the social realm. Its reversal and prevention requires that the operational objectives and actions of the prison are consistent with public expectations.

- If the prison refuses to gauge its performance by any other measure than recidivism, then accountability is little more than an illusion.

- No single event in history has had a greater impact on the prison's operations or ideological orientation than its recent growth.

- Stressed correctional institutions will seek to restructure themselves as a self-protective measure.

- Few government officials appear to understand the contention that the prison must measure its effectiveness not by expansion but by contraction. A decrease in its size and a diminishing need for its services should be the prison's only measure of success (since it relates directly to recidivism).

- The single biggest challenge that plagues the modern prison is a massive inmate population that necessitates all non-essential programs be reduced or eliminated in an effort to free up scarce resources.

- Expansion has always been associated with decreasing effectiveness and coldness. Contraction, on the other hand, has always been associated with an abundance of energy and warmth.

- Energy and resources are essential to the accomplishment of all tasks. If they are scarce, only the bare minimum is accomplished. If they are abundant and properly applied, anything is possible.

- A short-term sentiment does little to advance the causes of penology and works to the detriment of the offender and society by ensuring that only those challenges that demand immediate attention are considered essential. All other concerns, especially those pertaining to the future, receive little if any consideration.

- A generational approach promotes strict accountability.

- When an imbalance occurs, it produces a state of confusion and operational uncertainty whereby all institutional actions are reduced to their most basic denominator, and in the case of the prison, this has resulted in the warehousing of humans with little concern for how this approach impacts public safety.

- Balance requires harmony and interconnectedness between thought and practice. A continuing disjunction between the two would ensure that the prison is relegated to being little more than a warehouse. For an institution founded on hope and redemption, a failure of this nature is a condemnation of humanity in its entirety.

- We must remember that the only meaningful way to assess the prison's ability to act in a socially productive manner is through the measurement of recidivism. No other measure so directly or so succinctly reflects the ability or inability of the prison to promote public safety.

QUESTIONS

1). It was suggested that cycles or rhythms are found within the social realm just as they are in nature. Is this an accurate observation? Explain.

2). What effect does a negative inmate culture have on an amenable inmate's attitude toward treatment? How can the establishment of positive relationships facilitate offender reform? Do you think that the current inmate culture is as "open" about its defiance toward the authority of prison officials as was suggested within this chapter? Explain.

3). Do you agree with the statement that "the key to achieving most goals is to understand the nature of energy and how to apply it in an efficient and effective manner - and nowhere is this needed more than in corrections"? Explain.

4). What is the single most important measure of the prison's effectiveness? Explain. Are there additional performance measures that might provide added insight into its ability to safeguard public interests?

5). If the average citizen were to visit a prison, would he/she be appalled at the level of idleness among the inmate population? Explain. What is the relationship between idleness and continued criminality?

6). As a manifestation of their government, most citizens believe that the prison has their best interests at heart and acts accordingly. Is this an accurate observation? Explain.

7). How can confusion about goals and objectives hinder the use of energy within an institution? Explain.

8). How does isolation affect prison operations? Who are the prison's constituents and do they currently hold prison officials accountable for their actions or inactions? Explain.

9). What effect has expansion had upon prison operations? What potential effects would contraction have upon the prison? Is future contraction likely? Explain.

CHAPTER TEN
Ich Bin Feuer und Flamme Dafur

The innovative, creative and progressive thinker
is master of tomorrow; all others, merely spectators.

The title of this chapter is borrowed from a statement made by Albert Einstein in response to an invitation he received to join the Institute for Advanced Study, an academy designed specifically to facilitate innovative, creative and progressive thought. Einstein's utterance translates as, "I am full of fire and flame for it". Einstein's statement appears fitting since we have now arrived at the final chapter of this modest work and like those at the Institute for Advanced Study, we too believe that innovative, creative and progressive thought can solve persistent and perplexing problems while improving the human condition.

All authors and their readers eventually find themselves at a point where dialogue has run its natural course and each is left with his or her thoughts. As this point approaches, we as authors must undertake three tasks. First, we must provide a summation of what has appeared within the preceding pages; secondly, we must offer an assessment of what the future may hold; and finally, we must bid our readers farewell. Other authors generally approach these tasks in this sequence. However, since this book is intended to promote innovative, creative and non-conventional approaches, and since we have never been good at saying adieu, we will say it now and will do so out of sequence. It is our sincerest hope that you will find our ideas to have merit and that your future undertakings result in personal and professional fulfillment. Now to the précis.

There are a number of ways in which the material to follow can be presented. The most reasonable is to call attention to those ideas that we wish to emphasize. In doing so, we are aware that this is our final opportunity to make an impression. We want each reader to understand that the contemporary prison is in crisis. Prisons are overcrowded and many employees have abandoned any semblance of a professional orientation. Instead they have become increasingly transient in their ideologies, commitments and employment pursuits. Similarly, administrators remain more concerned about the management of large populations than about running their institutions in socially responsible ways. Add to this muddled concoction an inmate population that rejects correctional authority in all its various manifestations and you will likely form an appreciation for the current state of affairs. The prison is in crisis and any portrayal of it otherwise is either based on ignorance or is an intentional fabrication meant to mislead the public.

Prison Accountability

While we acknowledge that the prison has largely been powerless to control its growth, its officials have nonetheless reveled in their ability to operate with little or no accountability. For many years, prison administrators were trusted to act in the best interest of their inmate populations and the public. Most correctional officials took this responsibility seriously and acted accordingly. While accountability has traditionally been minimal, it nonetheless existed. Over time, the number of prisons grew as did their respective populations. Erroneously assuming that officials would act appropriately in light of these events, our courts adopted a hands-off approach whereby judges increasingly refused to become involved in the prison's affairs. This doctrine, still cited by the judiciary itself, has permitted the prison to operate with little accountability. Abuses of all kinds have become common. Institutions that operate free from public and judicial oversight are capable of great atrocities and the prison is guilty of doing just that. Recent social movements have called attention to government abuses including those occurring in the prison. With public pressure mounting, the judiciary has begun to selectively intervene in the daily management of our nation's correctional institutions. This has forced our prisons to remake themselves in order to meet humanitarian and constitutional standards. Prison officials have grudgingly made changes, yet many have been superficial and have had little effect.

As the twenty-first century approached, political and judicial processes became noticeably conservative in their handling of offenders. Politicians and scholars alike increasingly dismissed rehabilitation as a correctional objective, allowing punitive ideologies to gain a considerable foothold. As more offenders were incarcerated, prison administrators were increasingly rendered unmotivated and financially incapable of providing therapeutic programming. This led to a diminishing concern for the post-release behaviors of inmates. Without the humanizing effects produced by treatment, large inmate populations increasingly became more confrontational and defiant. This is reflected in a contemporary inmate culture that openly opposes all forms of government authority. The size of the inmate population affects every aspect of an institution's culture due to the intense competition that it creates for scarce resources, services and even personal space. The struggle to survive within a predatory and violent culture is now the primary objective of the contemporary inmate whereas the management of prisoners in a cold, sterile and industrial fashion is now the hallmark characteristic of the modern administrator. Each of these approaches fuels the other and neither contributes to the long-term safety of society.

So why are these observations relevant? This question reflects a healthy curiosity about the relationship between the prison and our lives. With so many offenders currently imprisoned, the chances that you will encounter a former inmate on any given day may be greater than you think. For example, if we take the estimated population of the United States (318,000,000) and divide it by the approximate number of prison inmates (1,700,000), we see that there is 1 prisoner for every 187 free citizens. This suggests that during a typical week, you or a loved one will work with, befriend or otherwise interact with an ex-inmate. Ex-inmates can be found in every community. They frequent the same parks that you frequent, shop in the same stores, and drive the same roads that you and your family traverse. This acknowledgement makes the prison's actions a bit more personal. Most citizens understand this and expect the prison to prepare inmates for life out here amongst us! If the prison is successful in doing so, fewer of us will fall victim. If the prison fails, then our risk of becoming prey increases dramatically. This is why offender rehabilitation should be recognized as the single most important pursuit of the prison. It is the only penal objective that contributes to the long-term stability of society.

There should be no doubt that officials are failing to take offender rehabilitation seriously. It is now common for inmates to joke about the revolving doors of the prison. These revolving doors depict the likelihood that a newly released inmate will be returning to a life of crime and incarceration posthaste. Behind the prison's fences there is an acknowledgement by all parties involved that inmates are being released without any preparation whatsoever. Inaction of this kind contributes to unnecessarily high recidivism rates. While contemporary rhetoric suggests that rehabilitation is still being pursued, in reality nothing could be further from the truth. This fact is recognized by both staff and inmates, alike.

Gesundheit

One way to improve the prison is to view it as a living organism. A biologically based perspective recognizes that unhealthy environments beget unhealthy individuals. An individual coming into contact with an unhealthy environment can, in turn, become sick. Social contagions can and do exist! Based upon work pioneered by Chicago-based scholars, this perspective recognizes that the prison's environment can have a dramatic effect on an inmate's post release behavior. A healthy environment that promotes personal responsibility, treatment and rehabilitation impacts post release behavior much more positively than does an environment where treatment is devalued and where idleness and predation are common. And while most offenders can be described as being socially unhealthy prior to imprisonment, it is the responsibility of the correctional institution to ensure that such a condition does not worsen, and when possible, improves.

While the prison is similar to other institutions, the degree of influence that its culture exerts over its populace exceeds that which is exerted by other institutions over their own clientele. The strength of this effect is derived from the prison's pervasive negativity and the forced interaction occurring between those found therein. By forcing amenable inmates into close proximity with those who are more criminally inclined, we guarantee the transfer of criminal techniques and perspectives. In essence, the prison has become an unhealthy institution where social contagions exist and are actively passed between residents.

To more fully understand this process, one must acknowledge that the prison is a socially isolated institution. As such, its culture is shaped almost exclusively by inmates, and in particular by those inmates who are the most predatory and violent in nature. These inmates have created an environment that bestows upon them status, influence and access to contraband items and services. This culture promotes an anti-establishment orientation that must be adopted by all inmates if they wish to win acceptance and obtain a minimum level of safety. Embedded within this ideology is the collective conviction that the criminal justice system is discriminatory, that its officials are corrupt and that opposition is warranted.

It has also been suggested that a community's culture is transmitted to its populace through a process of interaction and communication. If this occurs within larger society then how much truer is it for small, artificially created communities? This question suggests that correctional practitioners must determine the content of the message that they wish to send. Should this message be one that promotes social health or continued criminality? Furthermore, the likelihood of successful transmission increases with length of exposure. The longer the exposure, the greater the scope and intensity of transmission. It is interesting to note that prison sentences have grown longer over the past three decades giving us the lengthiest terms of incarceration in the industrialized world. This approach, originally intended to create a deterrent effect, may actually be proving counterproductive to the public's long-term safety since it permits transmission to occur over longer periods of time. Exposure of this nature increases the likelihood that transmission will occur and that it will have a detrimental effect on the behaviors of ex-inmates. This situation is not hopeless nor is it irreparable. In fact, evolutionary science suggests that the effects of de-evolution and decline can be reversed through deliberate and calculated action.

The Physics of Penology

When applying physics to penology, it becomes inescapably obvious that a consideration of Werner Heisenberg's work proves valuable. Heisenberg suggested that if it were possible to ascertain the location and the momentum of a particle (a feat that continues to elude physicists), a great deal more could be learned about the atomic realm. Although Heisenberg was interested in the behavior of particles, his insights apply equally well to the social realm. For example, penologists have an advantage over physicists since they can determine both the location of an offender on the criminal continuum (which ranges from first time to habitual offender) as well as the momentum at which an offender is gaining experience. This permits a determination to be made about the extent to which an offender has become invested in criminality and how likely he/she is to respond to treatment. For example, an inmate whose location and momentum are near the lower end of the continuum will, in all probability, be more likely to accept and benefit from treatment than those inmates positioned near the higher end of the spectrum.

It has also been observed that particles often become entangled. Physicists have known for many years that relationships between particles can become so strong that it is impossible to describe one linked particle without describing the other. The destinies of linked particles become inextricably and instantaneously connected regardless of their distance from one another or the environments in which they are located. This observation reveals the powerful effects that relationships have on behavior at the atomic level. These relationships affect the location, momentum and future behaviors of particles. If particles and prisoners are similar, then the relationships that develop within the prison may also affect the location, momentum and future behaviors of inmates. In fact, observations made at the atomic level appear to have their counterparts within the social realm. If this is true, then these dynamics can be manipulated to facilitate offender reform. For example, the promotion and establishment of positive institutional relationships might promote lawfulness among ex-inmates. Manipulations of this kind were evaluated during a study conducted at the Hawthorne Works Factory. It was during this study that environmental modification and peer influence were observed to produce positive changes in human behavior. These observations suggest that behavior is affected by environment and the relationships that develop therein. By modifying the prison's environment, practitioners can capitalize on these dynamics, minimize the negative effects of incarceration and promote the development of pro-social attitudes and behaviors that are essential to the long-term stability of society.

Insights can also be obtained by comparing the prison to the nucleus of an atom. An atom's nucleus serves as the central or unifying point around which particles congregate. The prison serves a similar function by making congregation and interaction among inmates possible. Furthermore, particles can be electrically charged. Protons are positively charged whereas electrons carry a negative charge.

It is for this reason that each can be compared to inmates who display a positive or a negative orientation toward treatment. For example, protons can be compared to those inmates amenable to treatment whereas electrons can be compared to those who oppose treatment. For the sake of this presentation, let's consider electrical energy and peer influence to be functional equivalents. As we learned previously, the flow of energy between particles is always from a negative toward a positive orientation. This suggests, if we stay true to our comparison, that peer influence also flows from a negative toward a positive orientation with negatively oriented inmates influencing those of a more amenable nature. If this is indeed the case, then the negative culture created and perpetuated by nonamenable inmates has a corrupting effect on those who are positively oriented. This, in turn, adversely affects future recidivism and crime rates.

Any consideration of energy and its flow requires a familiarity with the laws of thermodynamics. This proves essential to our effort since this law pays particular attention to systems, which for our purpose includes all correctional institutions. Since energy always seeks its lowest level and is constantly being transferred between systems and their environments, over time it dissipates. The energy that remains is then increasingly taxed and is used in less efficient and less effective ways. This is referred to as entropy. Entropy denotes a state of disorganization and confusion that inhibits the ability of a system to operate in an efficient and effective manner. When we consider the prison, it becomes evident that its current state of entropy is unparalleled. The prison is now completely characterized by its ineffectiveness at breaking the crime cycle. Furthermore, the exchanges of energy occurring between it and society (its environment) are highly controlled and are limited in scope. In essence, the prison devotes little energy toward treatment and operates with only modest levels of external interaction and review. When combined with the hands-off doctrine, this approach has allowed violent and predatory inmates to seize control of the larger inmate population ensuring that they too oppose treatment.

Equally insightful are the laws of motion. Accordingly, these laws stipulate that the direction and momentum of an object (or for our purposes a system) remain unchanged unless otherwise acted upon. And similar to the laws of thermodynamics which acknowledge the influence of energy on behavior, the laws of motion similarly recognize that increases or decreases in mass also produce changes in behavior. Changes wrought by large inmate populations have had a significant impact on the prison's ideology and its activities. To increase the prison's ability to break the crime cycle, we must understand how energy, entropy and mass converge to impact the correctional process.

To arrive at a greater understanding of the physical world, scientists have traced the origin of the universe back to its genesis event. For physicists this moment is known as the big bang. Penologists have similarly traced the history of the prison back to our nation's first correctional institution. Immediately following their creations each experienced an inflationary period when growth occurred exponentially. For the universe, a big bang suggests that at one time all matter was compressed into an inconceivably small point of infinite density and temperature. The big bang liberated this matter, creating time and space itself as material was propelled outward from the explosion. Everything that we observe today was a product of this event. As the universe continues to expand, energy will be spread ever more thinly across greater expanses of space. This leaves only a few possibilities with regard to the fate of the universe. For example, it may continue to expand, spreading energy ever more thinly. If this happens, the universe will eventually die a cold and dark death. Additional possibilities suggest that the universe may eventually contract. Whether this is a one-time event or a never ending series of expansion-contraction events remains debatable. Regardless, expansion can be considered a prelude to death whereas contraction is synonymous with energy, warmth and vitality.

But how does this observation apply to the prison? Well, the prison has itself undergone a series of expansion and contraction events. It is during periods of contraction where energy increases as does an interest in treatment and rehabilitation. It appears clear then that there is a rubber band effect observable within the social realm. A rubber band can only be stretched so far, a universe can expand only so much, and a prison can grow only so large before a situation is created that may result in disaster. Said a bit differently, there may be a self-healing mechanism at work in both the physical and social realms where expansion is inevitably followed by contraction. For the social realm, a state of decline, sickness and inefficiency may naturally be followed by a state of energy, health and vitality; and just as the bob of our pendulum swings first one way then the other, expansion precedes contraction and punitive approaches may eventually give way to treatment.

Predictions

The material presented herein easily lends itself to predictions about the prison's ultimate fate. There are two methods of presenting these predictions that prove beneficial. The first of these deals with the anticipated nature of the future prison in the event that expansion continues; the second involves the expected actions of the future prison in the event of contraction.

In the event of continuing expansion, we can expect:

- inmates to be given progressively fewer opportunities to participate in productive activities. As the prison's mass increases, decreases in energy and resource levels will result in fewer social and therapeutic programs. An inverse relationship exists between the size of the inmate population and the number and types of programs offered,

- the prison to provide fewer amenities, increasingly offering only those items and services absolutely necessary for the subsistence of the inmate population,

- added limitations to be placed on inmate communications and interactions with the outside world. An inverse relationship exists between the size of the inmate population and the frequency, duration and quality of contact that it will be permitted to have with the public,

- entropy to increase as reflected in mismanagement, chaos and unnecessarily high recidivism rates,

- job satisfaction and a professional orientation among staff to plummet,

- staff to become more transient in their employment practices resulting in a workforce that is increasingly hesitant to invest in the correctional process. As such, prison violence will rise and humanitarian and operational standards will suffer,

- inmate leadership to increasingly operate in an open and defiant manner that relegates prison officials to the periphery of facility management. This will doom the prison's culture to continuing degradation that will ultimately result in a situation whereby officials have little choice but to negotiate with powerful inmates to ensure the security of their facilities,

- amenable inmates to find it increasingly difficult to withstand assimilation into the prison's culture. This will require them to openly acknowledge the authority of inmate leaders and pledge their support to these regimes. This will result in fewer inmates being able to maintain their amenable orientations,

- recidivism rates to remain unnecessarily high or perhaps even increase, and

- officials to hesitantly seek alternative approaches to incarceration. These alternatives will likely include the use of technology to confine offenders to their homes, to particular areas within a community or to communities created specifically for this purpose (whether these approaches will slow or halt expansion remains doubtful).

Expansion, if it continues, will result in the prison's demise. If the physical and social realms are governed by a similar set of laws, then expansion can produce no other outcome. Continued expansion will produce an extremely cold, impersonal and sterile institution that devotes little effort toward inmate betterment. Instead, diminishing levels of energy will increasingly be used to provide only the basic necessities. Concerns will turn to addressing the immediate needs of the inmate population including food, clothing and the provision of utilities, and less toward the future needs of the inmate or society. In an attempt to offset the mounting costs associated with incarceration, there will be attempts to make prisons self-sufficient and even profitable. Increased entropy will result in a state of chaos, discontentment and inmate objectification that the prison has not previously experienced. Prison officials will increasingly have little choice but to negotiate directly with inmate leaders in an attempt to maintain control. Little hope will exist for that portion of the inmate population that is amenable. Amenable inmates will be targeted for exploitation, victimization and even servitude. There is little doubt that at some point the situation will grow so dire that alternatives to incarceration will be sought. These alternatives will rely heavily upon technology as a means to detain inmates in non-institutional settings including their own homes, in certain areas within their communities (perhaps zoned for inmate presence) or even within special communities designed specifically for offenders. It is doubtful that these approaches will slow or halt expansion. Instead, they will likely widen the net of correctional control.

In the event of contraction, we can expect:

- the prison to provide an increased number of opportunities for inmates to participate in productive and personally rewarding activities. In essence, as the prison's mass decreases, rising energy and resource levels will result in the provision of additional therapeutic programs,

- the prison to provide an increased number of opportunities for inmates to communicate and interact with the outside world. As the prison's mass decreases, the frequency, duration and quality of these interactions will increase,

- decreased entropy and the adoption of more effective and efficient management practices,

- job satisfaction and a professional orientation among staff to improve,
- staffing trends to stabilize with employees becoming less transient in nature. A staff that invests in the correctional process will seek to reduce violence and adhere to humanitarian and operational standards,
- inmate leadership to lose its stranglehold over the prison's culture. This will reduce the ability of powerful inmates to control the prison's populace, and
- recidivism and crimes rates to fall.

While we wish to avoid presenting an overly optimistic view of the future prison, we remain convinced that reducing its mass is in the best interest of society. If the physical and social realms are in fact governed by a similar set of laws, then contraction would prove beneficial. Contraction would encourage practitioners to change the way they view inmates. For example, treatment requires that practitioners view inmates as unique individuals. As such, the objectification of the inmate population would decrease, promoting a similar orientation among prisoners who often objectify each other and their victims. By approaching inmates as unique individuals, prison officials can help counter this dynamic. Individualized treatment would become the norm. An increasing amount of energy and resources would be earmarked for inmate betterment. And while there will always be a necessity to meet the immediate needs of the inmate population, there will emerge a realization that preparing inmates for future release and reintegration is the best way to promote the long-term interests of society. In essence, short-term objectives will be augmented with an interest in undertaking a course of action for the long-term betterment of society. There will also be an increasing realization that there are at least two types of inmates within the prison, each with its own orientation. This realization will lead to an increased effort to separate these groups, eliminating the possibility of contact and entanglement. There will also be a growing awareness about the negative effects that the prison's culture and its unique form of peer pressure have on offender behavior. Once energy levels increase, entropy decreases, staffing levels stabilize, and attempts are made to rehabilitate amenable inmates, we will experience lowered recidivism. In essence, the effectiveness and the efficiency of the prison will increase as it is freed from the crushing effects of a large inmate population.

Conclusion

There you have it, a few progressive, innovative and creative ways to approach penology! Again, we are in no way suggesting that humans are incapable of exercising free will. Instead, we are simply suggesting that there is a value in looking at one's area of specialization from an interdisciplinary perspective. In doing so, a fresh viewpoint can be obtained. The fields of criminal justice and penology are relatively new academic disciplines and as such, we want to ensure that they don't stagnate any more than they have already. It remains our sincerest wish that readers will build upon the foundation that we have provided herein and take our approach to the next level. Furthermore, we acknowledge that our approach can be applied to the broader criminal justice system and to other institutions including those associated with health care, education and social services.

HIGHLIGHTS

- The prison is in crisis and any portrayal of it otherwise is due to ignorance or is meant to mislead the public.
- Any institution that is permitted to operate free from public and judicial oversight is capable of great atrocities; the prison is guilty of doing just that.
- The size of the inmate population affects every aspect of an institution's culture.
- Predation and a struggle for survival are the hallmark characteristics of the modern inmate.
- The management of prisoners in a cold, sterile and industrial fashion has become the hallmark characteristic of the contemporary administrator.
- Offender rehabilitation is the only objective that contributes to the long-term stability of society.
- A healthy environment that promotes personal responsibility, treatment and rehabilitation impacts post release behavior much more positively than does an environment where treatment is devalued and where idleness and predation are common.
- While the prison is similar to other institutions, the degree of influence that its culture exerts over its populace exceeds that which is exerted by other institutions over their own clientele.
- The prison has become an unhealthy institution where social contagions exist and are actively passed between residents.
- If influence flows from a negative toward a positive orientation with negatively oriented inmates influencing those of a more amenable nature, then the culture existing within the modern prison must have an adverse effect on future recidivism and crime rates.
- The prison is now completely characterized by a level of ineffectiveness that is reflected in its failure to break the crime cycle.

- To increase the prison's ability to break the crime cycle, we must understand how energy, entropy and mass impact the correctional process.

- A rubber band can only be stretched so far, a universe can expand only so much, and a prison can grow only so large before a situation is created that may result in disaster.

- An inverse relationship exists between the size of the inmate population and the number and types of programs offered.

- An inverse relationship exists between the size of the inmate population and the frequency, duration and quality of contact occurring between inmate populations and society.

- Future incarceration may include detaining inmates within their homes, in certain areas within their communities (perhaps zoned for inmate presence) or even within special communities designed specifically for inmate populations. It is doubtful that these approaches will slow or halt expansion. Instead, they will likely widen the net of correctional control.

QUESTIONS

1). Do you believe that the prison is in crisis? Why or why not?

2). How might the size of the inmate population affect a prison's operations? How might the size of the inmate population affect an institution's culture? Give specific examples to support your responses.

3). Do you agree with the observation that while the prison is similar to other institutions, the degree of influence that its culture exerts over its populace exceeds that which is exerted by other institutions over their own clientele? Explain your response and be specific.

4). Are there natural limits to prison expansion? Explain. Are there natural limits to its contraction? Explain.

5). What additional predictions could you offer in the event of continued expansion?

6). What additional predictions could you offer in the event of contraction?

APPENDIX

Term	Physical Description	Penal/Social Equivalent
Big Bang	The moment the universe came into existence.	The moment America's first prison was created.
Cosmic Inflation	Expansion of the universe.	Expansion of the prison system.
Electron	A sub-atomic particle with a negative electric charge.	An inmate displaying a negative orientation toward treatment.
Energy	The ability of a physical system to complete a task.	The prison's ability to break the crime cycle.
Entropy	The inability of energy to be used effectively or to be transformed from one form into another.	The inability of the prison to use energy to promote the long-term interests of society.
Gravity	An attraction between objects.	A shared pursuit that binds individuals or groups to a common objective (i.e. rehabilitation).
Mass	The total amount of matter that exists within an object.	The overall size of the inmate population.
Nucleus	An atomic point around which actions and movements occur.	The penological point around which actions and movements occur (i.e. the prison).
Proton	A sub-atomic particle with a positive electric charge.	An inmate displaying a positive orientation toward treatment.

BIBLIOGRAPHY

Arntzenius, Linda. *Institute for Advanced Study*. Charleston, SC: Arcadia Publishing, 2011.

Black, Henry, and Harvey Davis. *Practical Physics*. New York, NY: Macmillan Publishing, 1922.

Blackburn, Ashley, and Shannon Fowler. *Prisons Today and Tomorrow* (3rd ed). Burlington, MA: Jones and Bartlett, 2012.

Bernfeld, Gary, David Farrington and Alan Leschied (eds). *Offender Rehabilitation in Practice: Implementing and Evaluating Effective Programs*. New York, NY: John Wiley and Sons, 2001.

Blomberg, Thomas, and Karol Lucken. *American Penology* (2nd ed). Piscataway, NJ: Transaction Publishers, 2010.

Brian, Denis. *Einstein: A Life*. New York, NY: John Wiley and Sons, 1996.

Burgess, Ernest, and Robert Park. *Introduction to the Science of Sociology*. Chicago, IL: The University of Chicago Press, 2011.

Checkland, Peter. *Systems Thinking, Systems Practice*. Hoboken, NJ: John Wiley and Sons, 1981.

Courtillot, Vincent. *Evolutionary Catastrophes: The Science of Mass Extinction*. New York, NY: Cambridge University Press, 1999.

Craig, Leam, Louise Dixon and Theresa Gannon (eds). *What Works in Offender Rehabilitation: An Evidence-Based Approach to Assessment and Treatment*. West Sussex, UK: John Wiley and Sons, 2013.

Cullen, Francis, and Cheryl Jonson. *Correctional Theory: Context and Consequences*. Thousand Oaks, CA: Sage Publishing, 2011.

Dirac, Paul. *The Principles of Quantum Mechanics*. Oxford, GB: Oxford University Press, 1930.

Feynman, Richard, Robert Leighton and Matthew Sands. *Six Easy Pieces: Essentials of Physics Explained by its Most Brilliant Teacher*. New York, NY: Basic Books, 2011.

Foucault, Michel. *Discipline and Punish: The Birth of the Prison* (2nd ed). New York, NY: Vintage Books, 1995.

Garland, David. *Punishment in Modern Society: A Study in Social Theory*. Chicago, IL: University of Chicago Press, 1993.

Gideon, Lior, and Hung-en Sung. *Rethinking Corrections: Rehabilitation, Reentry, and Reintegration*. Thousand Oaks, CA: Sage Publications, 2011.

Goldsmith, Donald, and Marcia Bartusiak (eds). *E=Einstein: His Life, His Thoughts, and His Influence on Our Culture*. New York, NY: Sterling Publishing, 2006.

Handbook on Classification in Correctional Institutions. New York, NY: American Correctional Association, 1947.

Johnson, Lee. *Experiencing Corrections: From Practitioner to Professor*. Thousand Oaks, CA: Sage Publications, 2012.

Joos, Georg, and Ira Freeman. *Theoretical Physics* (3rd ed). New York, NY: Dover Publications, 1986.

Kaku, Michio, and Jennifer Thompson. *Beyond Einstein*. New York, NY: Penguin Random House, 1995.

Kellert, Stephen. *Borrowed Knowledge: Chaos Theory and the Challenge of Learning Across Disciplines*. Chicago, IL: University of Chicago Press, 2008.

Kiel, Douglas, and Euel Elliot. *Chaos Theory in the Social Sciences: Foundations and Applications*. Ann Arbor, MI: University of Michigan Press, 1997.

Latessa, Edward, and Alexander Holsinger (eds) (4th ed). *Correctional Contexts: Contemporary and Classical Readings*. New York, NY: Oxford University Press, 2011.

Licht, Deborah, Misty Hull and Coco Ballantyne. *Psychology*. New York, NY: Worth Publishing, 2014.

Mach, Ernst. *Popular Scientific Lectures*. Chicago, IL: Open Court Publishing, 1910.

Mann, Charles, and George Twiss. *Physics*. New York, NY: Scott Foresman and Company, 1910.

Mears, Daniel, and Joshua Cochran. *Prisoner Reentry in the Era of Mass Incarceration*. Thousand Oaks, CA: Sage Publications, 2015.

Monahan, John. *They Called Me Mad: Genius, Madness and the Scientists Who Pushed the Outer Limits of Knowledge*. New York, NY: Berkley Books, 2010.

Morris, Norval, and David Rothman (eds). *The Oxford History of the Prison: The Practice of Punishment in Western Society*. New York, NY: Oxford University Press, 1998.

Myers, David, and Nathan Dewall. *Psychology* (11th ed). New York, NY: Worth Publishing, 2015.

Newton, Isaac. *The Principia*. Amherst, NY: Prometheus Books, 1995.

Paley, William. *The Principles of Moral and Political Philosophy*. Whitefish, MT: Kessinger Publishing, 2008.

Reviews of Modern Physics (v. 20, n. 1): New York, NY: American Physical Society, 1948.

Reviews of Modern Physics (v. 30, n. 3): New York, NY: American Physical Society, 1967.

Robinson, Andrew (ed). *Einstein: A Hundred Years of Relativity*. New York, NY: Metro Books, 2010.

Ross, Jeffrey, and Stephen Richards. *Beyond Bars: Rejoining Society after Prison.* New York, NY: Alpha Books, 2009.

Tewksbury, Richard, and Dean Dabney. *Prisons and Jails*. New York, NY: McGraw Hill, 2009.

Turner, Jonathan, Richard Machalek and Alexandra Maryanski (eds). *Handbook on Evolution and Society: Toward an Evolutionary Social Science*. New York, NY: Paradigm Publishers, 2015.

von Boehm, Gero. *Who Was Albert Einstein?* New York, NY: Assouline Publishing, 2005.

INDEX

ABOUT THE AUTHORS

Curtis R. Blakely, associate professor, holds a bachelor's and master's degree from the University of Nebraska, a specialist degree from the University of Central Missouri, and a doctorate from Southern Illinois University. Dr. Blakely teaches at Truman State University and has served as a probation/parole officer, a prison classification officer and as a police-training specialist.

Michelle L. Blakely holds a bachelor's degree from the University of South Alabama and a master's and doctorate from Auburn University. She specializes in program evaluation and has an interest in delinquency prevention and treatment. As Director of the Disability Services Office at Truman State University, Dr. Blakely ensures that students have the opportunity to participate in all aspects of the Truman experience. Dr. Blakely formerly served as faculty at the University of Connecticut.

The Blakelys are active in both the criminal justice and physics communities and have donated items of historical significance to Xavier University's Department of Physics, the Niels Bohr Library and Archives and to the Great Library in Alexandria, Egypt.